CANDY

A Tea Party With The King Continues ...

by

Elizabeth Foy

Candy

by Elizabeth Foy

Printed in the United States of America

ISBN 9781615793242

Edited by Lynda Shively-Linn

Illustrations by Anna Buttitta

www.xulonpress.com

Preface

*E*lizabeth Foy has brought God's words of healing grace to my heart for more than twelve years now. She has spoken His love and power into my life through her sermons, her teaching, her counsel, and her prayers. Now she has begun to bring His great mercies to me through her writing.

Along with Victoria, I experienced the sweetness of the King's love in *A Tea Party With The King.* Now, I am able to watch with Candy as the King brings healing to hurtful relationships. As I read I felt the King's love enter my own heart, preparing me to receive the King's healing for myself.

I have found that our King uses Elizabeth's parables of the kingdom almost as He uses Scripture, to touch deep places in our hearts and fill them with His love. As I read *Candy* the words seemed to go down as smooth as cream, sweetening my whole life in the process.

I pray that you enjoy reading *Candy*, and that the healing love of the King fills your life as you read.

Helene Walker
Advisory Board Member, **Highways & Hedges Ministries**
Charter Team Member, **The KING'S Tea** (SM)

Foreword

*R*eading through *Candy*, my thoughts traveled back two thousand years ago, when Jesus Christ left an incredible assignment for every believer – that of personally sharing the "Good News". Sadly, far too many disciples hold a distorted image of how they should accomplish this task, envisioning a complicated process of that which should be the natural outflow of our daily walk with Him. So, how then are we to witness?

Woven into the fabric of this simple story are delightful turning points which portray the analogy of "Kingdom Business," and thus illustrate various ways through which one may fulfill the Lord's command. As Candy and her friends discover, bearing witness to our personal relationship with "the King" need not be cumbersome. And like me, you may also find yourself exclaiming, "Hey! This applies to me!"

John & Patty Probst
Authors of *The Strangers & Pilgrims Series*

Acknowledgements

*W*riting a book with limited technical resources can be very taxing. So, once again, my heartfelt thanks go to Lynda Shively-Linn for steering me through the maze of editing the content and preparing this manuscript for publication.

Yet would this monumental task have been accomplished were it not for the love and patience of Dr. Jan Harbuck, Vice President of **AEGA Ministries**? My "boss lady" graciously allowed the use of office facilities to complete most of the process. And then – on the night prior to leaving for a conference, and in the midst of flooded offices and electrical outages – she found time to upload graphics for the book. What a friend!

Finally, Ray and I extend our heartfelt appreciation to AEGA President & General Overseer, Dr. Henry Harbuck, for his insight and uncommon wisdom shared with us on countless occasions. "Brother Henry" and Jan provide continuing encouragement to the various outreaches of **Highways & Hedges Ministries**.

Loving HIM and You,
Elizabeth Foy

Dedication

$\mathcal{F}$irst of all, this book is dedicated to my husband, Ray. He is the one who, like Jesus, knows me best and continues to love me anyway.

Then, to all of those (too numerous to list) who have enriched the development of God's nature in me, walking with me through all the adventures of my life. You refused to let go of me, never holding my weak moments against me as I searched for my footing in each season God has brought me through. My love and gratitude go out to you. You continued to believe that, like Candy, the ungodly attitudes of my heart would be overcome by HIS love; and that eventually, the good would outweigh the bad. Each of you has joined me in recognizing that those things God does in our lives are done that many may be blessed. We, like Candy, have learned that in HIS upside down Kingdom, the weak are used to lead the strong.

God bless each of you, as you have certainly blessed me!!!!

Table of Contents

*D*o you ever wonder if your actions influence the lives of others – perhaps altering them in either positive or negative ways? Is there really such a thing as everyday people transforming the environment around them? Can our decisions (or lack thereof) affect those around us, and those in our future?

In the second volume of the *A Tea Party With The King* series, Victoria's friend Candy takes the gentle truths acquired in the tea room and molds them into a life pattern that impacts many. Faced with many of the friends (and foes!) she knew as a schoolgirl, she and her acquaintances discover that emotional wounds don't have to remain gaping and sore — they can be healed from the inside out at the table of the King!

Watch with me as a once shy schoolgirl, now a caring and influential woman, ignites her community and sets in motion events that change the direction of a city, transforming the lives of its residents. And it all began with a cup of tea in the presence of the King.

-1-

"*How* Beautiful!"

The feelings in Candy's heart were so strong the words leapt out of her mouth without restraint. Looking out the kitchen window, her heart rejoiced at the early signs of spring. She always looked forward to the departure of winter and the new life that sprang up with the warmth of the bright sun. She suspected her love for spring was because it was this time of year when she'd met Victoria many years ago. In fact, she could hardly believe so much time had passed since that eventful day. Yet here she was — a grown woman now, with children of her own. How differently things would have been had it not been for her chance meeting with Victoria that day!

Yet as much as she wanted to linger at the window watching the early arriving birds find their way to her feeder, she really had much too much to do! In only a few days, the King would return to the city and there were still many tasks on her "to do" list in preparation for His arrival. Candy smiled to herself at the thought. It was almost as if the arrival of spring had timed itself to coincide with His return, and that nature was rejoicing with her.

-2-

*L*et's see … there needs to be a thorough cleaning of the Gathering Room. And, of course, the tea room will need to be gone over with a white glove inspection. After all, it was there she'd had a life changing experience with the King. Yes, many things could go by the wayside, but not the tea room. With that in mind, she decided to make it her first stop of the day. After that there would be time to go to the market, purchase items for the Gathering, and put flowers in the front beds of the King's house.

Making her way up the steps of the King's house, her mind replayed a day many years ago – the first time Victoria had taken her to meet the King. Candy smiled, remembering how very nervous she'd been, and how hard she'd worked to hide her feelings. Had she known who and what awaited her behind these beautiful wooden doors, she would have realized there was nothing to fear.

Taking the last few steps two at a time, she pulled on the handle of the entrance doors. Pausing inside, a great sense of peace and well being seemed to wrap itself around her. Truly amazing! The same reaction enveloped her each time she entered His house. Even when He was not physically present, there was a sense of Him in this house. And though it was true she always felt Him near her, the feeling certainly intensified when she entered His house.

A brief look at the Gathering Room revealed the ladies appointed to clean were already hard at work. The chairs were neatly arranged and there was a podium in place for the speakers. Fresh ferns had been placed in baskets, and a small table just right for a pitcher of water set ready for the meeting. And now to the tea room! Of course, she could have asked the same ladies to tidy the tea room, but Candy just could not bring herself to do it. No, she loved going there and dusting each chair and table. It was a joy, not a burden, to take down and launder the curtains. In fact, that was today's task; so with ladder in hand, she began climbing up and re-hanging the beautiful floral drapes in the tea room. It was just as she was deciding how many chairs should be brought in and calculating the amount and types of cookies Barbara needed to make for the Gathering, that she was caught off guard by the presence of someone entering the room.

Without turning, she *knew* who had entered. His presence literally filled the room. As she stepped off the ladder, she turned to face the King, His warm smile making her heart leap with joy.

"Well, Candy, I see you are about my business, as usual."

"Oh yes sir," she replied. "The city has been in such a stir about your arrival. In fact, how were you able to make it here without a crowd following?"

"I knew no one would be expecting me at night; so I arrived last evening, and have been resting today. However, the bustling of all those cleaning ladies you set upon my house awakened me."

"Oh my, if I had known you were arriving early, I would have had this work done days ago," Candy began to apologize.

"Please, Candy ... do not think I am complaining. You can't imagine how pleased I am when I arrive unexpectedly to find my citizens busy about the Kingdom's business with no prodding. You are very faithful, and I really appreciate all you do for me," the King said, taking a seat at one of the tables.

Following his lead, Candy seated herself across from him.

"This sure brings back memories, doesn't it Candy?"

"It certainly does!" she replied. "Just this morning I was remembering how it was about this time of year when we met many years ago."

"Tell me Candy, how are things at home these days? How are your parents? And, of course, I need an update on Eric and the children. Not that I fear they are being neglected, in the least. You are a wonderful wife and mother, you know."

Candy blushed slightly, considering his words. When she evaluated her performance in those areas she saw only shortcomings. And of course any mention of her parents always brought mixed emotions. Certainly things were much better than in the past, but they were not as perfect as Candy would have liked them to be. How to begin?

"Well, sir, my father is really much better now. But days when there is a lot of stress in his life I know he would like to go back to his old ways. Yet thankfully he has not."

"It has not been an easy path for him," the King replied quietly. "It is hard to break free of habits you have had for a long time."

"I realize that now that I am older," she responded with more compassion than in earlier years. "I know he never wanted to be unkind to mother and me. It was as if he was caught in a trap and could not get out. I wish I had understood that earlier. Perhaps I could have been more help to him."

"One thing I am sure of, Candy," the King went on, "he has always known you loved him. In fact, it was at this very table that you and I first talked about him, remember?"

"How could I ever forget? The second day I came here with Victoria you went straight to the heart of the matter. You asked why I always kept my head down, and you told me that I should never carry the shame for someone else's behavior."

"And that was when the flood of tears began," the King reflected. "You were afraid you had not done a good job of keeping your family secret. But truly, I was the only one who could look into your heart and see the sadness."

"Thankfully, because of your kindness and love for me and my family, my father no longer has a problem with alcohol. He is now a happy and helpful member of the Kingdom," Candy smiled. "In fact, when I looked out the window this morning, he was already busy mowing the lawn and picking up trash that had blown onto the property. I think he enjoys being able to give back in some small way for the joy he has experienced since coming into the Kingdom."

"And as for Eric and the children," she continued. "They are fine. I think Eric works too hard, but the children are growing like strong trees. They will be here for the Gathering. They wouldn't miss it for the world."

"I will be glad to see them, as well," the King smiled.

"Oh my, look at the time, sir. There are still so many things that must be done before the Gathering. The people are quite excited, you know. Your arrival seems to bring life to everything around us. In fact, I believe the cardinals in my garden arrived early this spring just so they would be here during your visit." With that, Candy asked the King's permission to leave and went about her way.

As Candy left the tea room, the King sat in silent reflection, a serene sense of joy evident on his face as he surveyed the quiet room. So much had happened here, events that had shaped — even changed — the course of many lives. He recalled the first day he had met Victoria. And the day she had reached beyond her fears and began to ask others, like Candy, to come to tea. A gentle smile crossed his face. Victoria! Such a contradiction in natures! On one hand, a shy girl very afraid of what others thought and said; yet at their first meeting she had been relaxed, and not hesitant to speak her thoughts. Yes, it would be good to see all the girls together again. This was going to be a great Gathering.

-3-

*C*andy would certainly have to hurry now. She had not meant to spend so much time at the King's house. But when he arrived, how could she not stay for a visit? It had been such a long time since she and he had been alone. This evening she would be able to tell Eric and the children that he had arrived and she had spoken with him.

As she entered the market, her eye was caught by a beautiful little girl. She did not recall having seen her before. Several years younger than her own daughter, Karen, the child seemed very outgoing and curious. In fact, she walked straight up to Candy and introduced herself.

"My name is Lydia. What's your name?"

"My name is Candy," she said, smiling at the straightforwardness of the child.

"That's a funny name for a lady," Lydia responded, a quizzical expression playing across her face.

Laughter sprang from Candy's lips as she remembered Victoria had voiced the same thought many years ago. "Yes, I guess it is not a very common name. You see my mother wanted a daughter very much and she prayed that the daughter would be thoughtful and sweet to others, so she chose the name Candy for me."

"Oh, that makes sense," Lydia agreed.

"What are you doing here today?" the child asked.

A gentle nudge reminded Candy that this was an opportunity to tell Lydia about the Gathering. "I am on a very important errand," she said. "I am in charge of preparing the King's house for the Great Gathering. There are many things that must be purchased, and I always find the freshest fruit and healthiest plants at this market. Since I want only the

best for the King, I am here to make my purchases."
A big smile spread over Lydia's face. "My mother
and father own this market," she beamed with
pride.

"Then I am fortunate indeed to have made
friends with someone who has connections with the
owners," Candy laughed. Lydia seemed pleased with
that, sensing she had stumbled upon some source of
importance.

As Candy made her way through the market
carefully examining each item, Lydia followed close
behind. She seemed puzzled why so many of the
items were returned to the tables and shelves after
Candy looked at them. After a period of time, her
curiosity got the best of her. "What is wrong with
the things you put back?" Lydia asked. "My daddy
is very careful about what he puts in our market.
Don't you think his produce is good?" Lydia asked,
rather defensively.

Candy brought herself out of deep thought. "Now
Lydia, didn't I say the reason I come here is because
of the quality of the products?"

"Oh yeah, I forgot," Lydia answered. "It's just that my mom has been sick lately and there have been a lot of medical bills. We are trying to sell as many things as possible to pay the bills."

"Well Lydia, I am being very careful of my choices because I want everything to be perfect at the Gathering with the King," Candy explained.

"He must be hard to please," Lydia surmised.

"Nothing could be farther from the truth," Candy quickly corrected. "He is pleased each time one of his citizens does their best. He always compliments us because he knows how difficult it is for us, as citizens, to see things the way a King does. When he knows we are doing our best to be faithful citizens, he is always quick with a word of encouragement and love."

"Love?" Lydia asked in disbelief. "That's not what I've heard some people say."

Just as Candy was about to respond to Lydia's misinformation concerning the King, Lydia's mother called her to come inside. They said their goodbyes and Lydia ran quickly to her mother's side. Yet as Candy turned back to the task at hand, she could not forget the look on the child's face when she had told of the King's love for those in the city. She really wished Lydia's mother had not called her at just that moment. 'Oh well,' she said to herself, 'I will give that more thought after I attend to the Gathering.' But deep within her heart she could hear the King's voice whispering 'Kingdom business, Candy'.

-4-

*C*andy stepped back with the sense of a job well done. Each plant was properly placed in the flower beds. They looked fresh and expectant just like the faces she had seen while completing her errands at the market. 'My, it is really getting late. I should be on my way. The children will be home from school soon and there is dinner to prepare,' Candy reminded herself.

As she picked up her gardening tools, the King appeared on the sidewalk. "Everything looks great, Candy. This place really shows all the work you have put into it. I hope you know how much I appreciate you."

Candy looked up, her eyes reflecting the love in the King's eyes. "Sir, it is my joy to do these things for you. Each time I come here I leave with a sense of completion. It is as though each thing I do has real value to you."

"It is not *only* the things you do at my house that please me Candy," the King began in a sober voice. "Like today ... you took time to speak with Lydia about me."

"My goodness," Candy began, "it is just as Victoria always said. You really do know everything that happens in the city. And I could have sworn I even heard you speak to me while I was at the market."

Hearty laughter burst from the King. "My beloved Candy, are you referring to the moment when I whispered that Lydia was a part of the Kingdom business I wanted you to take care of?"

"Then I didn't imagine it!" shrieked Candy.

"No, Dear One. You have grown so close to me that our hearts and minds are becoming as one. So when you come upon a situation like today at the market, your heart immediately searches out my thoughts about it. And in your heart you hear my intentions."

"I have often heard Victoria speak of hearing you everywhere she went, and of sensing your presence at all times. I can hardly believe I am able to do the same."

"Candy, it is my desire for all citizens of my Kingdom to come to this reality. But we must talk about Lydia."

Yet just as she was about to surrender to a deep conversation Candy remembered the time. "Sir, if you please, I cannot stay now. My children will be waiting for me," she said with a measure of regret, gathering her garden gloves.

"Off you go, then. It can wait for another time. Give Eric and the children my love. Tell them to stop by for a visit if they have time." And with that Candy gave the King a great hug, picked up her tools and headed toward home, walking briskly to avoid being late.

-5-

*T*hank goodness! Just as Candy started up her street the children were beginning to walk up the front steps. She called for them to wait for her. Arriving breathless, she greeted Karen and Brett with a smile that showed them she must have had a great day.

"How are you two doing?" she asked, unlocking the front door. "Was school good today? Brett, how did your book report turn out? I prayed this morning you would be able to present the report with confidence and clarity."

While Brett felt he was getting old enough not to give an account of his daily activities, he was secretly pleased that his mother was interested in him. In an odd sort of way it was comforting to know she kept his activities foremost in her mind, and always believed for the best possible results.

"It went really well today," he answered. "In fact, when I sat down after giving my report, I realized speaking in front of the class doesn't make me as nervous now as it once did."

"What about me," Karen interrupted. "Don't you want to know my grade on the science project?"

With only a slight rebuke in her tone Candy responded, "You know I do, Sweetie. It is just that you don't seem to have as much trouble speaking to a group as your brother, so his report came to my mind first."

As Candy entered the kitchen and began putting her gardening tools away, she looked at both children and realized how grateful she was for them. While they were quite different from each other, they were both very gifted. Yes, she and Eric were blessed indeed.

Looking at the clock on the wall, she told the children she must start dinner and they should be about their homework. As she stood with the refrigerator door open staring mindlessly at its contents, the back door opened. In walked Eric, a full half hour earlier than expected. While she was pleased to have him home, she laughingly scolded him in a loving voice. "Leave it to you. The one day I'm late getting home and forgot to make any preparations for supper, you come home early."

Pretending to be offended, Eric picked up his briefcase. "Fine. I'll go back to the office until a more convenient time."

But as he made his way to the door Candy stepped in front of him, laughing. "Not so fast! Now that you're here, you can help me think of something for supper."

"Well, from the bags on the counter, it appears you have been to the market. So, let's just have a nice salad for supper. That should be easy."

"That does sound easy, and very healthy. In fact, I remember last week freezing the extra vegetable soup. I'll get that out. And with the salad, even the children should be filled."

As Candy retrieved the soup from the freezer, Eric could not resist one last jab. "Could it be that you had important people take up more of your time today than you had planned?"

"How did you know?" Candy spun around, making a 180 degree turn in seconds.

"I have been married to you long enough to know who puts that light in your eyes, and that smile of radiance on your lips," Eric teased. "He is here, isn't he? The King has already arrived."

Nodding, Candy took a long look at her husband. He really was the kindest, most understanding man she had ever met. Well, except for the King of course. "Yes, he is here. I can't believe it shows that plainly."

"As organized as you usually are, my dear, it was easy to see that no supper preparations translated into 'the King has arrived'," Eric countered.

As they set about preparing supper, Candy told Eric how plans for the Gathering were progressing. As she recounted the events of the day, she was reminded of Lydia. "Eric, when I was at the market today I met the sweetest little girl. Her name is Lydia. She is so friendly. She came right up to me and introduced herself. She told me her parents owned the new produce market. You know … the one that opened a couple of months ago."

"I know the one you are talking about," Eric answered as he sliced tomatoes. "I believe one of her parents may have lived here as a child, and they have only recently moved back … perhaps to be near family. The wife has been ill and has needed help with the child while her husband worked. In fact," Eric considered a moment, "I think they should be about our age. How old is the little girl?"

Candy thought for a moment. "Oh, younger than our children. She looks about kindergarten age. So I must be older than her mother. But I wonder if I would have known either of them in school."

Just as she was about to quiz Eric for more of what he knew, their children entered the kitchen as if they were starving.

"When can we eat?" Brett asked.

"Yeah, we're hungry," Karen chimed in. Putting the finishing touches on the soup and salad, Eric and Candy sat down with them to enjoy, not only a tasty meal, but the sharing of the day's events.

-6-

$\mathscr{A}$s part of her duties for the Gathering, Candy was going about the city visiting with each citizen to invite them to the special event. While this might sound like a burdensome task, Candy enjoyed it greatly since it gave her an opportunity to visit with friends she did not see regularly. And it was a chance to see people in their very best mood. After all, most everyone was excited the King had arrived.

It was on one of these occasions that Candy saw Lydia again. As she began walking down Primrose Lane, she noticed Lydia playing alone on a nearby lawn. Approaching her, she reflected on the street's lovely name, and how it spoke of bygone days. Once this street had been where many well-to-do citizens had lived. The houses were new, and the lawns manicured to perfection. But during a time of rebellion against the King and his statutes, the area had suffered much financial ruin. Now the houses looked unkempt and sad, and the lawns appeared to produce more weeds than flowers. It seemed that once the rebellion had been put down, those who seemed intent on disobeying the King had chosen to remain here, leaving the remainder of the citizens alone.

Normally Candy would not have entered this neighborhood on Kingdom business, yet somehow she now felt almost compelled to visit each house. And although she still intended to knock at every door, she decided to skip the first few houses and head straight for Lydia.

"Hello Lydia, remember me? I'm Candy, and we met a few days ago at the market. How are you doing?"

With a voice not quite as confident as in their first meeting, Lydia acknowledged that she remembered Candy. And looking into her eyes, it was easy for Candy to see that something was troubling the little girl.

"It seems something is wrong, Lydia. Would you like to tell me about it?" "Oh, it is just that my mother is having a bad day," she began, with eyes beginning to tear up. "She is very weak. My dad asked me to stay home so she would not be alone until he finished working."

As Candy was about to give a meaningless response to Lydia, she heard the King's voice whisper, 'Kingdom business, Candy'. "Perhaps I should go in and check on her," Candy suggested, prompted by the nudging in her heart. Pleased to have a new ally in the battle, Lydia jumped up at once; and taking Candy's hand, led her up the sidewalk and onto the front porch. As Lydia opened the door she called out, "Mom, I have a friend with me!"

It did not take super sonic hearing to recognize the heavy sigh that came from the bedroom. And for a moment, a chill ran down Candy's back at the sheer weariness she heard in that long exhaled breath. "Lydia, haven't I told you I am not well enough for you to have friends over?" the tired voice asked. But although the voice sounded very tired and very old, Candy realized that it also sounded familiar in an odd sort of way.

"Don't worry," Candy called out, making her way down the hall. "I will only be here a moment. I met your daughter recently and she wanted me to meet you."

As they entered the dark bedroom, Candy could see the only light was a small lamp across from the bed. The curtains were tightly drawn, and she felt as if even the furnishings wished she would go away and let the woman rest. Quietly she and Lydia ventured further into the room, not knowing fully what to expect. Her eyes adjusting to the dim light, Candy made her way to the side of the bed.

"Hello, my name is Candy" she began, once again taken aback by the seeming familiarity of the woman. "I don't normally make a habit of entering where I have not been invited, but your daughter is hard to refuse."

At the mention of Lydia, a gentle smile crossed the woman's lips and she struggled to sit up in bed. Straightening up to obtain a clearer view of her visitor, a small gasp-like sound came from the woman's lips. "Candy, is it really you? I can't believe it. It has been years since I have seen you." With more strength in the voice and a better view of her face, Candy now understood why the woman seemed so familiar.

"Patty? I can't believe it's you. Do you mean that Lydia is your daughter? This is remarkable. I guess I should have noticed in the beginning. But the first day I met her I could not see you clearly when you came out of the market to call her home. I don't know why I didn't put it together earlier. She really does have your eyes, you know."

But after the initial joy of having an old friend show up at her home passed, Patty began to fidget nervously. It was apparent that she suddenly remembered how she looked and the untidy condition of the house. A blush of embarrassment seemed to cover her face.

"I must look a mess, Candy. I haven't been well lately, and this house has really gotten dirty. Ken and Lydia do as much as they can — but with working at the market, Ken has limited time. And, of course, Lydia is too young to do much," her voice trailed off.

"Don't worry about that," Candy soothed. "I can see that I have caught you at a bad time. I was just trying to visit each home in town to tell everyone about the Gathering with the King. I can see that you are not feeling well, and you might not be able to attend, but I wanted you know about it."

Lydia pulled on Candy's arm, "What's a Gathering?"

Candy looked at Patty to see if she would approve of an explanation. In a very tired voice Patty said, "We'll talk about it later, Lydia. Miss Candy has a lot of people to see, and she probably needs to be going now."

With a downcast face, Lydia let go of Candy's arm. Candy's heart went out to the little girl. She could only imagine how much Lydia would enjoy the Gathering. She was certainly the type of person who would be right at home in a crowd of loving, laughing people. But she sensed from Patty that she should leave now.

"Well, I will be going now. Patty, I hope you feel better soon. If there is anything I can do to help, please let me know. In fact, if it's alright, I will check on you again in case there is something you need."

"We will be fine," Patty responded with more confidence than Candy thought was real. "Ken and Lydia manage quite well together, and I'm sure I will be up and around in a few days."

-7-

*I*t was later that evening, after the children were in bed, that Eric and Candy sat enjoying the quiet of the living room. Her favorite time of day, Candy always felt so at peace to simply sit with her husband and discuss the events of the day, or their dreams for the future. But tonight the heaviness in her heart would not go away.

"Eric, I made calls on Primrose Lane today," she began.

"Really? Isn't that a little out of the way of your usual calls?"

"Yes. But I kept thinking if the people in that area would attend the Gathering, then perhaps some of the anger and sadness still left from the rebellion could be done away with at last."

Putting his newspaper down, Eric turned to look at her. "There's something bothering you. What is it?"

Taking a deep breath Candy began. "You remember a few days I told you I met a little girl at the market."

"Yes, I do. If I remember correctly, you told me her name was Lydia." Candy could not help but smile. That was her Eric, remembering all the details. He paid such close attention when she and the children told him things. Their lives, thoughts and problems were so important to him.

"That's right, her name is Lydia. As I made my way down Primrose Lane today, I saw her sitting on a lawn.

"Uh, just a moment, Candy. Shouldn't she have been in school today?" Candy smiled again. Always majoring on details. Nothing escaped Eric's notice. "Yes, that's part of the problem. She called to me and I went over to speak to her. It seems her mother was particularly weak today and there was no one to stay with her. Her father had asked Lydia stay home from school in case her mother needed something. When I spoke to her, she invited me inside to meet her mother."

"Well that had to be a good thing," Eric interjected, "so why the long face tonight"?

"Eric, you won't believe who her mother is!" the words came rushing out of Candy's trembling lips.

"She is Patty. Patty Hawkins!" For a moment Eric looked at Candy in disbelief. He had never met Patty, but he recalled that Patty had been the source of a lot of pain for Candy in her younger years. And for just a moment, Candy seemed, once again, to be the young girl tormented by unkind words instead of the strong, confident woman he knew as his wife.

Eric moved closer to Candy on the sofa. "Tell me about the visit Candy. It is evident that it has shaken you more than you realize."

"Eric, I don't know where to begin. When I first realized who she was, I felt small and insecure again ... the same way I did years ago at school. But when I looked around the room and saw how pitiful she looked, like a small wounded animal hidden beneath the bedding, I felt a twinge of joy. Can you believe it? Me. A grown woman. Someone who has committed her life to helping the King. Someone to whom he has entrusted the Gathering. I actually had to fight feelings of happiness that she was suffering. I'm so ashamed." With that confession the tears began to flow.

Eric reached for a tissue to dry Candy's eyes. "It has been a long time since you have seen Patty. I am sure if you had been prepared to meet her, you would not have had such a reaction. You would have had time to work through the feelings in your heart toward her before going to her home."

"Eric, I know you are trying to make me feel better. But don't you see? How could these feelings have been hiding in my heart all these years? Surely they should not be there. I feel like such a failure," the words were spoken through quivering lips.

Just as Eric was about to make another attempt at comforting Candy, the doorbell rang. 'Who on earth could that be,' Eric thought. It was too late for guests to come by. "I will answer the door and send them on their way," he told Candy, heading toward the front door. But as he pulled on the door handle and prepared to curtly dismiss the person standing on the other side, he was surprised to see the King!

"Oh, it's you, sir. I didn't expect you. Forgive me. Please, come in."

When Candy saw the King enter her living room, she quickly sat up and tried to straighten her face. The King strode past Eric and took the seat next to Candy on the sofa.

"Child, there is no need to try to hide those tears. I felt your heart breaking this afternoon. I had hoped when you left Patty's house you would come straight to me. Why didn't you?"

Candy shook her head, too embarrassed yet to speak. How could she explain? How could she tell him about the dark thoughts she'd had today? How disappointed he would be in her. Surely he would feel as if he had wasted all these years with her. She was sure he would have nothing more to do with her when he realized how dark her heart was.

But as Candy fumbled to find words, the King moved closer to her on the sofa and took her hand. As he did, his sleeve moved up revealing the long, deep scar on his arm. Candy's eyes immediately fell on the scar. As if reading her thoughts the King spoke, "Don't be bothered by the scar Candy. It doesn't hurt, and is always a good reminder of how things turn out when my citizens choose to rebel against my statutes."

Candy's voice was soft as she spoke. "I know why you have the scar, sir." It was years ago when an enemy of yours in this area began to tell people that you were unkind. He convinced many citizens that your statute to send 10% of their funds to support the Kingdom was wrong."

"Yes, Candy, that was an unfortunate incident. I was wounded in a skirmish. But thankfully the rebellion was put down, and most of the citizens recognized the truth of the statute."

"Yes, once they realized the funds were stored in the event any of them came into need, the matter was resolved, Candy reflected.

"All citizens except for those on Primrose Lane came into obedience with the Kingdom statute," the King said, a hint of sadness in his voice.

"Primrose Lane," Candy sighed.

"Yes," the King began, "because of their unwillingness to participate in the program, when the drought came and the crops failed affecting everyone, they had no where to turn. They ended up suffering needless loss and disappointment. Let's talk about Primrose Lane, Candy."

"Sir, I remember as a child longing to be one of the lucky ones who lived there. But when I saw it today … it is such a sad street. And there is hopelessness everywhere. In fact, when I approached Lydia's home I had forgotten it was the house Patty had lived in. Perhaps if I had remembered, I would have been better prepared to see her again," Candy pondered.

"I believe it is good that you were unprepared for the meeting, Candy," the King said gently. "It is at such times that you often see the state of your heart most clearly. Today you had an opportunity to see something buried deep within you."

"It is something I could have done without knowing," Candy responded.

"I disagree," the King gently rebuked. "You have always wanted to be everything you could possibly be, Candy. Since we met you have only desired to please me and to advance my Kingdom. Don't you think it is important to know if there are any traces of the past still lingering within you?"

"I suppose so," Candy agreed hesitantly. "But why did I enjoy seeing Patty in such a position?"

"There is something in everyone that desires to ensure evil deeds are punished. People believe it brings justice to situations or circumstances they consider unfair," he explained. "But Candy, what if the things you have thought … or done … or said … received the 'justice' others might say is deserved?"

With that statement, Candy looked at both the King and Eric. In truth she responded, "Sir, it would be terrible. I have thought some very unkind things about people in my life. And I have certainly made some awful choices. Eric knows better than anyone that I am not a perfect person. I would hate for the people of the city to judge me by my worst moments."

"That is true, child. But my love has declared you worthy, and no one can say otherwise. My love has also declared Patty worthy, but she is having a hard time understanding it. Life has not been as wonderful for her as you might imagine. Give her time. Give her a chance. I think you will find her to be a decent person," the King said.

"I will, Sir." Candy committed, dabbing the lingering tears from her eyes. "I told her I would check on her, and I will. I will do my best to make things better for her."

"I believe that in giving of yourself, you will find a friend in Patty. In fact, there are many things you have in common. But we will leave that till later. For now, know you are loved and forgiven of any shortcomings," the King smiled, rising to leave. "I will leave you in Eric's capable hands for now. Have a good evening."

After the King left, Candy and Eric talked for a long while. She told him about all the events of her day and he encouraged her, sharing some ideas on how to approach Patty and her family. As chairman of the Community Outreach Center, he felt there might be help available for Patty. If so, Lydia could attend school daily like other children, no longer obligated to stay home and care for her mother. Delighted by Eric's thoughtful recommendations, Candy's heart overflowed with love. How thankful and blessed she was to have such a loving husband.

-8-

*T*wo days had passed since Candy first visited Patty in her home. There was not much on her schedule and since she had promised to return, why not do it today? Starting down Primrose Lane, Candy thought again about the uprising against the King's statute concerning giving into the Kingdom. It always amazed her that everyone could not see the wisdom in it. After all, hard times happen to everyone sooner or later; and it was good to know the King held a reserve for just such times that His citizens could draw on.

Yet it was plain to see by the condition of the houses lining the little street that disobedience brought ruin. According to the statute, those who had not contributed to the fund could not draw from the fund. And when the financial setback hit the community, the wealthy people living here had no where to turn in need. They had trusted only in themselves, and had been unable to rebuild. It was truly a sad sight indeed.

Slowly she made her way up the steps. Not knowing what to expect on the other side of the door, she gently turned the doorknob and called out, "Patty it's Candy. Are you up to visitors today?"

To her surprise a cheerful voice responded, "Of course, come in. We are glad you have come."

As Candy entered the hall and turned into the bedroom she was startled. "Victoria!" she exclaimed. "What are you doing here? When did you arrive?"

Making her way toward Candy, the room filled with the sound of Victoria's laughter. "Slow down a minute. I can only answer one question at a time." She reached out, enveloping Candy in a warm embrace — the embrace of a friend too long away from someone they care deeply about. Releasing Candy from her hug, she stepped back to get a better look. "You look wonderful. I can see life with Eric and the children has been good for you. Why, you absolutely glow," Victoria exclaimed.

Candy could only look into Victoria's deep hazel eyes, taking in the pure love that shined there. Could this confident, loving woman possibly be the quiet, shy girl who had spoken to her so long ago on the school playground? "Yes, life is very good, Victoria. And I can see from the glow on your face that things are good for you as well."

"Yes," Victoria responded as she led Candy toward the bed, "things are going well. But I am sure you came to visit Patty, not me. Why don't the two of you visit while I put on the kettle for tea?"

Candy took a seat near Patty's bedside. Smiling nervously, she suddenly realized she could not think of anything to say and silently wished Victoria had stayed a bit longer. "Well, how is Lydia doing?" she finally asked, staying in safe territory.

"Oh, she is wonderful, Candy," Patty said in a voice that sounded truly happy Candy was there.

"It was so thoughtful of you to take time with her. I worry sometimes that she has had to assume too many adult duties because of my illness. She certainly seems to have taken a liking to you. She has often asked when you would be coming back."

"She's a lovely child, Patty. You have done a wonderful job raising her. Like you at her age, she doesn't seem shy about anything and seems to have an opinion about everything," Candy complimented.

"Well, I certainly hope she grows out of some of my traits," Patty replied with assurance. "Those traits did not do much for me it seems." Just as Candy was about to inquire further into the meaning of her remarks, Victoria returned with the tea tray.

"It seems you two did not miss me at all," she teased. "Let's share a cup of tea together. I have found it's a wonderful way to set friends at ease and open conversation." As Candy helped herself to a cup of tea she looked thoughtfully at Patty. There was more life in her face today. Perhaps, Candy surmised, this was one of her 'good days'. Yet, at the same time, she sensed it might also have something to do with Victoria's presence.

After a couple of hours of girl talk Candy felt she should go. After all, there were still some chores she had left undone, and the children would soon be home. As she rose to go, Victoria suggested she would walk Candy out. Leaving the bedroom, Candy turned to say goodbye to Patty. While she was beginning to look a little drained, she also had a contented expression on her face.

"Patty, I'll see you later," Candy promised.

"I look forward to your return," Patty gathered the strength to reply. And with that, Candy and Victoria walked outside.

"How long have you been in town?" Candy asked her old friend. "Does the King know you are here?"

Victoria put her arm around Candy's shoulder, "Yes, he knows. In fact, he is the one who asked me to come early for the Gathering and spend some time with Patty."

Candy looked at Victoria questioningly, "Why didn't you let me know you were here? Eric and I would have had you over for dinner, or at least for a good chat. You know the children would love to see you."

"And I would love to see them as well," Victoria answered. "But Patty had become so weak the King thought no time should be wasted in attending to her. So I came straight here after stopping first to visit with mother."

"I will have to give Barbara credit for being an excellent secret keeper," Candy chimed in. "I have seen her several times this week, and she never mentioned a word about your being here."

Victoria giggled to think of she and her mother working together again on a project for the King. Times like this always reminded her how the King had healed the broken relationship between them. It was nothing short of a miracle that the mother and daughter who once had little in common (and even less to say to each other!) were now close friends.

"Candy," Victoria's voice took on a more serious tone. "It is important for us to reach out to Patty now. In fact, if you have time, it would be beneficial for you to speak with the King concerning Patty."

"We spoke briefly the other night," Candy answered quietly, remembering her feelings.

Almost as if reading her thoughts Victoria responded, "Candy, you are a wonderful citizen of the Kingdom and the King is very proud of you."

Seeing the look of love in Victoria's eyes, Candy nodded, agreeing to return as often as possible to visit with Patty.

-9-

"*Y*our gardens look lovely."

Candy spun around suddenly at the sound of his voice. "Sir, what are you doing here?"

"I came for a visit so you and I could discuss some things without interruption. There are workers in and out of my house today and I knew it was still a couple of hours before the children would return from school."

"Certainly, please come inside. I will make us some tea. I was ready for a break anyway, and you give me a great reason to stop weeding." Despite her upbeat tone, however, Candy felt a twinge of nervousness.

As she poured tea into the cups, the King got right to the subject. "How did your visit go with Patty?"

Candy sat down, choosing her words carefully, "I was surprised to see Victoria there. It was wonderful to be with her again, but I admit I was surprised. I don't recall Patty and her being close in school."

"It would be strange if you did," the King responded. "Like you, Victoria was not in Patty's social circle."

Candy could not resist her reaction, "That is an understatement. The days she was not ignoring us, she was telling lies about us."

"I see you are still working through your feelings regarding Patty," the King quietly chided.

"I don't recall you mentioning Patty coming to the tea room, sir. When did you meet with Patty?" Candy questioned.

"This may take a while to explain," the King sighed. "I am sure your memories of Patty are of a self confident girl, totally in charge of everything, someone who commanded strict loyalty from her companions, right?"

Candy reflected a moment, and agreed the King had described Patty to a tee. "Things are not always as they appear, are they Candy? If I recall correctly, many people mistook your shyness for arrogance in grade school."

With a blush of embarrassment, Candy dropped her head. "You're correct, sir."

"Like you, Patty had issues no one knew about," the King said. "There were problems in her home that would have surprised many citizens. Patty dealt with her pain the only way she knew how. She wanted to make sure the people around her were as unhappy as she was, so she made every effort to find their weaknesses." The King continued, "Do you recall when the rebellion began, and things went badly for the people living on Primrose Lane?"

"Yes, I do. In fact, wasn't it about that time when Patty suddenly disappeared? Her mother said she had gone to live with relatives, but I always wondered about that."

"People are very good at keeping secrets when they feel they have no choice," the King observed. "I will tell you something that only Victoria and I know. You must keep it close to your heart, Candy. But perhaps knowing the facts will help you see Patty in a different light. What you and others did not know was that while appearing on the outside to be a kind and successful business man, Patty's father had a very dark side. Consequently, he dealt with his insecurities by lashing out at Patty and her mother. When things did not go well in business or with his cronies, he became very violent with Patty and her mother. It was a dark secret they were afraid to share with anyone. When the rebellion was finally put down and he lost all his finances, he became even more violent. It was at that point Patty decided to leave. One evening, without warning, she left home … and did not return until recently."

Candy hardly knew what to say. Could this be the answer to so much of what she had wondered? While Patty had seemed very popular at school, Candy could never remember anyone ever being invited to her home. She had noticed this because her own father's drinking meant she had never been able to invite anyone to her home either. And it did seem there were times when Patty was especially unkind to herself and others. Could it be those days had followed unusually difficult nights at home?

"I see from your expression that things are beginning to come together," the King commented. "The same way others misjudged you, you have misjudged Patty."

"I see that now," Candy answered with genuine regret. "But where has she been all these years? And why did she come back?"

"To make a long story short, she ran to a city a great distance from here. At first, she did not know what she was going to do. While her father had been unkind, at least she had always had a home and food. However, being on her on, she was afraid and uncertain how to begin. After a few days of wandering the streets, she came upon the idea of how she could provide for herself. She began to apply for positions to clean houses, or to watch children for working parents." Candy's eyes got as big as saucers. The picture of Patty tending other people's children and cleaning their homes was mind boggling. Patty? With her perfect hair and perfect nails and perfect clothes? This was a lot to take in. "Candy, sometimes life doesn't give you many options. Patty was searching in the only places she thought she could succeed," the King said in a slightly corrective tone.

"Since my Kingdom covers great distances, there was a woman in that city who was a loving Kingdom citizen. She came upon Patty's application and knew immediately it was a part of Kingdom business." Candy smiled at the thought of others hearing the voice of the King in their heart directing their daily activities. The King continued, "Soon she had Patty settled in her home. While it took some time for Patty to get the hang of daily chores, loving the children came naturally to her. She seemed determined they would know only love and encouragement. She determined they would never fear having anger vented upon them. As time went on, the lady of the house asked Patty if she would like to attend a meeting with her and the family."

"It was a tea party, right?" Candy interjected.

"No, not a tea party ... but a Gathering," the King explained. "Very guarded at first, Patty began to relax as each person shared from their heart that day. She came to understand she was not the only person who had issues to overcome. Gradually she began to settle into the community and became an active part of the Kingdom there. About this time she met her husband, Ken. Shortly after that, Lydia was born."

"If things were so great there, why did she come back?" Candy wondered aloud.

"After a time she felt she needed to make things right between herself and her parents. She knew they had worried when she left so suddenly. One day she asked me about returning to make amends. It was very hard to tell her that her father had passed away due to his drinking, and that her mother had moved away and told no one where she was going. That news seemed to take a toll on her health. It was then she began to have days where she could hardly get out of bed. In desperation, she asked Ken if he would consider moving here ... to her home. Hoping the new environment would boost her health, he agreed. He is quite a good merchant and felt he would do well in business no matter where they lived. So they returned. I believe deep in Patty's heart she was hoping she would find her mother waiting for her."

"I guess things did not improve as Ken had hoped. I can't see that being here has done anything for that family," Candy observed sadly.

The King smiled, "That's where you are wrong. Just seeing you again and having Victoria visit has done much to increase her strength. And Lydia has taken quite a liking to you, you know."

At the mention of Lydia, Candy had to smile. She was such a bright girl. She was sure Karen would enjoy meeting her. A slight shadow crossed Candy's face, "It's a shame her mother was not here to receive her."

"Yes, that is most unfortunate," the King agreed. "But you can see now why it is important that you keep your promise to visit."

"Don't worry, Sir. I will not let you down," Candy promised, looking out the window. But before either of them could speak another word, the door opened and in burst Karen and Brett. Sheer joy spread across their faces at the sight of the King seated in their kitchen.

-10-

"*W*ow," Brett exclaimed, "I can't believe you're here. Look Karen. The King is in *our* house!"Karen giggled nervously. She was not accustomed to seeing the King outside of his house, except sometimes at a distance when he attended to business matters in the city.

"Come children," the King greeted, "tell me about your day." Taking their seats at the table, they chatted happily about school and friends, their voices rising and falling with excitement. Candy listened in as she prepared a snack for them, pleased at how freely the conversation flowed between her children and the King. While her cheery kitchen was not a tea room, they certainly seemed comfortable discussing matters of the heart with him. Placing the sandwiches on the table, she slipped out to complete her unfinished weeding of the garden, leaving the three of them alone to continue their visit.

As dusk began to fall, the King emerged from the kitchen to say he was leaving. "They are great children Candy," he complimented. Looking deeply into his eyes, Candy thanked him, assured that he was not just making polite conversation.

"Sir," she posed, an inquiry arising in her mind. "I noticed the same freedom today in my kitchen that we enjoyed together in the tea room years ago. But I had assumed such depth of conversation could only occur there."

"There is a simple reason for the companionship you witnessed," the King replied. "Each generation of citizens has the opportunity, if they choose, to step into relationship with me at the level their parents have achieved. With careful nurturing, that relationship can then deepen and be passed to the next generation." Caught off guard by this explanation, a puzzled look crossed her face.

"If this were not the case," the king went on, "then each generation would have to start at the beginning. Thus, the truly deep things of the Kingdom would never be discovered."

"But what happened between you and me, and you and Victoria?" Candy searched.

"Think of it this way, Candy. Victoria's mother had once enjoyed friendship with me, but walked away. Yet because of that initial relationship, it was easy for Victoria to accept me. Thus, she began her relationship with me where her mother had left off. On the other hand, neither of your parents had ever desired to know me. So, in your case, we had to start from the beginning. Remember how cautious you were at first? Victoria did not have this basic mistrust because her mother had, at one time, known me to be trustworthy."

While this was a lot for Candy to take in, deep within her soul she began to see the truth of it. Though her children were unaccustomed to seeing the King in their home, they did not hesitate to go to him, openly discussing their life experiences. She realized this was because, in a sense, she had gone before them and prepared the way.

"I see now. It is like leaving an inheritance to someone you love."

"Very much like that," the King agreed. "You developed this inheritance for your children in the tea room. And because of the genuineness of our relationship, it was easily conveyed to your children. Have a good evening, Candy. Give Eric my love." And with those words, he was gone.

"What have you been up to?" Candy asked, glancing up from her dinner preparations to look at her husband. For some reason, Eric looked especially pleased with himself this evening.

"Just a little Kingdom business," he grinned. "But seriously Candy, I did look into the matter of getting help for Lydia's family."

Candy's eyes lit up with joyful expectancy, and a feeling of overwhelming affection for her husband. The Outreach Council certainly had a great leader in Eric. She remembered many times when people stopped them in the street, asking him to review a matter. Highly ethical and conscientious, he always reported back to the person any information he learned.

"What is available?" Candy questioned. "They're so new in town that I've been concerned they might not qualify for any real help."

"The fact that they are new arrivals appeared, at first, to be a problem. But then I remembered any established citizen with a good record of giving to the Kingdom could use funds credited to their account for newcomers — provided the situation warranted it, and the giver was in agreement, of course."

"Okay, break that down in plain English for me," Candy laughed. "How does all that translate into help for Lydia?"

"Simple," Eric continued. "You and I can take some of the funds the King has collected from us for future needs and apply them to Patty and Ken's situation."

Candy stopped her food preparations and looked up blankly at Eric. "Let me get this straight," her tone was hesitant. "We have faithfully put funds in the King's treasury in the event our family had an emergency or the Kingdom suffered loss ... and you want to use this to help Patty and her family?"

"It's the only way, Candy," Eric said flatly. "Either we help them, or they don't get helped."

Candy's thoughts were suddenly whirling, memories from long ago rushing through her mind. Once again, she heard those cruel words spoken in her youth, and the demeaning looks that caused her so much pain. Surely Eric couldn't be serious. Could he? Her own husband wanted to take the security they had faithfully put away for their family ... and give it to Patty!

Eric waited quietly, watching the struggle on his wife's face. Finally, she dropped heavily into a kitchen chair, still without comment. Realization dawning, he suddenly recognized this was going to be more difficult for Candy than he had originally anticipated.

"Candy, what's wrong?" he finally spoke. "I thought you wanted to help Lydia. I've researched the entire matter, and this is really the only way to get the help her family needs. What do you think?"

Candy looked up, still struggling with her emotions. Then she heard it … 'Kingdom business, my child' and the words continued to repeat themselves in her mind. She took a deep long breath. "If you say this is the only way we can help Lydia, then we must do it."

Eric reached out and squeezed her hand, his face beaming with love. "I never doubted for a moment you would make the right decision," he said.

"Why is it that doing right can be so hard at times?" Candy questioned.

"I don't know," Eric replied thoughtfully. "All I know is that we certainly feel better when we do." He looked around the room, as if listening. "Where are those children of ours? They sure are quiet. I'd better check on them while you finish dinner."

-11-

The following day Eric began securing help for Lydia's family, petitioning the King to release funds from his and Candy's Kingdom account for Patty and her family. With the release of funds, he was able to obtain the services of a Kingdom citizen to go several days a week and clean for Patty. The lady would ensure that before she left each day there was a healthy meal ready for Ken and Lydia, and that all their clothes were clean and neatly put away.

It had been a few days since Candy had first seen Victoria at Patty's house. Today would be a good day to stop in and visit with them both. Happily,

Candy made her way down Primrose Lane. Though the neighborhood was still in disarray, there was an unusual feeling in the air. Candy couldn't quite put her finger on it, but something was definitely different. Even the air did not seem to hang so heavily over her head today.

Making her way to the door, Candy stopped suddenly. Was it her imagination or weren't these steps about to fall in the last time she was here? No, it wasn't her imagination. This wood looked new. 'I wonder where that came from,' she thought, stepping onto the porch.

Before she could knock on the door or turn the knob, the door began to open. In shocked disbelief, Candy found herself looking into the face of an old friend. "Barbara! What are you doing here?"

Barbara smiled, a gentle laugh escaping her lips. "I guess I am the last person you expected see here."

"Indeed you are. In fact, I was expecting to find your daughter."

"Well, that would be difficult. She's not in the city at this time. The King had business for her elsewhere, and off she went." Candy noted the look of pride on Barbara's face when she spoke of Victoria. She wondered if Barbara knew of the Kingdom principle she and the King had spoken of in her kitchen. Did Barbara realize that she was, in part, responsible for the great influence Victoria carried in the Kingdom?

"Come now, don't stand in the door. Patty will be glad to see you," Barbara encouraged, leading the way to the bedroom.

Candy was happy to see that today Patty was not lying in bed. Fully dressed, she was sitting by the window, and the draperies that were once tightly closed were now pulled open. Everything looked neat and orderly, albeit still old and worn. Yet there was a sense of sophistication all the same — quite a contrast to her last visit.

"Candy!" Patty's tone was welcoming, as though she were the lady of a great house. "I can't believe you have taken time for me today. I know things must be in such a hustle as the day of the Gathering draws near. Sit and have a cup of tea with me. I want to hear everything that is going on. It seems like ages since I was out of the house. But with Barbara's great cooking, I will soon be strong enough to walk Lydia to school, and perhaps even help Ken in the market."

Taking her seat across from Patty, Candy reflected on the changes bursting out around her. In fact, she was not sure that she was comfortable with this "new" Patty. In an odd sort of way, it occurred to her that perhaps she had felt more at ease with the weak and tired Patty.

At just that moment, Barbara returned, carrying a tray laden with a lovely tea set and a plate of cookies. "My Goodness, Barbara! Did you empty the pantry? There is enough here for a dozen people," Patty laughed.

"I knew you girls would enjoy a nice, long talk … so I made enough to keep your strength up," Barbara teased, leaving them alone again.

Patty looked out the window as Candy poured their tea. Taking the steaming beverage, Patty brought her thoughts back into the room. "I have so much I want to say to you Candy, yet I hardly know where to begin."

"I guess when in doubt, start at the beginning. At least, that is what Eric always tells me," Candy advised trying to quiet her own nervousness.

"Eric is right," Patty said, with a sigh. "I really should start at the beginning. I guess it's a good thing Barbara made lots of tea and cookies."

Candy settled herself more comfortably into her chair. She was not sure what Patty was going to say, but she knew it was important, and that she needed to listen quietly to her.

"First, I need to say I am sorry, Candy. When I think how cruel I was to you and others, I cringe. How could I have been so thoughtless? I guess when you are young, and you are disappointed or have been hurt, you lash out at the nearest person. Again and again, I've thought how you and others must have felt because of things I said. In fact, to simply say 'I'm sorry' just doesn't seem to be enough. But there is nothing else I can do. I can't go back and undo what has been done. I only hope you can find the strength for forgive me."

'Strength to forgive' Candy thought, 'is exactly what I need.' But the thought had no sooner left her mind than she felt enveloped with the King's presence. Suddenly it was as though her heart had wings. She looked more closely at Patty. The woman before her was nothing like the girl who had made her life miserable at school. There was depth and substance to the woman sitting across from her. How could she hold the deeds of that frightened, hurting young girl against this woman?

"Patty, I do forgive you," she said, her voice almost breaking. And in that moment, as the words of release poured forth, it was hard to tell which woman felt more free — the one asking forgiveness or the one granting it. Suddenly, they were both crying and laughing at the same time; and it was almost as though the years had rolled back and they were young schoolgirls again.

Just then the front door opened and Ken and Lydia walked in. "We could hear the laughter from the front lawn," Ken chided. "What's going on in here?"

"Oh, just two old friends catching up on lost time," Patty responded as Ken bent over to give her a hug.

"Hi, Lydia … do you remember me?" Candy asked.

"Of course I do," Lydia replied in her most grownup voice. "You are my new friend that I met at my daddy's market."

"That's right," she smiled back at the child. "Oh my, look at the time," she said, arising. "I need to be going home to prepare some of your daddy's produce for supper."

Candy smiled to herself as she made her way up Primrose Lane. Her visit with Patty had been a good one, and a glimmer of hope had arisen in her own heart after their heart to heart talk. Yet as she left the small family behind, she couldn't help wondering what lay ahead for them.

-12-

It was only a few days until the Great Gathering, and Candy felt as if she was nearing some sort of countdown. Different from a normal Gathering, citizens from nearby towns and cities were coming together to make one great event. And since for many the distance was too great to travel in a day, Candy had made arrangements for these attendees to stay with local citizens. She had just completed her final check of the accommodations when she was summoned to the King's house.

As she entered, Candy felt a little like a schoolgirl called to the principal's office. Mentally, she checked off items on her 'to do' list. Yes, each item was taken care of. To her mind, everything seemed to be going well. Nevertheless, she knew he would not have called her if it were not important. 'Oh well, you'll never know standing here outside the door' she scolded herself. And in she went.

"I'm glad you came so quickly, Candy," the King said graciously. "I know time is short to have everything set in order for the Gathering. However, just today I was made aware of a problem, and I need your help."

"What is it sir?" Candy anxiously inquired.

"Ken stopped by to see me on his way to the market this morning," the King began.

"Is something wrong?" Candy began, her heart rising to her throat. "Is Patty alright?"

"Yes, yes. Patty is fine. In fact, that is part of the problem," the King puzzled.

"Ken was talking with her this morning, telling her how happy he was that she would be well enough to attend the Gathering. Yet when he brought up the subject of the Gathering, Patty became very withdrawn. She said she did not think she would be able to attend. Ken was stunned! He asked if she had begun to feel badly again, but she told him truthfully that it was not because of her illness. She told him she did not believe she could face all the people who would be there."

"But, why ever not?" Candy asked in disbelief. "I thought she was the one so determined to move back. Why, Ken didn't even know anyone here. It was at her insistence that he came. That's just like her! Always having her way! It's not fair!"

"Whoa, young lady. Hold up a moment. I did not ask you here to find fault with Patty. I need you to help me convince her to attend. It appears you still have some unresolved feelings regarding Patty which must be dealt with," the King lovingly corrected.

"You're right, Sir." Candy dropped her head in shame. "Every time I think all is forgiven and put behind me, something crops up."

"We can take care of that now," the King extended his hand to her. "You know, Candy, forgiveness is not a feeling that you have. Rather, it is a commitment you make. So when you choose to forgive — and remember it is one of the Kingdom statutes to do so — you are making the decision to release hurts from the past. Then when old memories or feelings about something or someone return, as they often do, say to yourself, 'I will not think on that, and I will not hold that against them.' Remember, forgiveness is a choice — not a feeling."

"I see that now," she began. "I thought that I would be overcome with love for Patty and that's how I would know I had forgiven her. I see now that it is a process, not just an event, and it will take time and effort on my part."

The King nodded. "Now that is behind us," he said. "Go and visit Patty, and see if you can convince her to attend the Gathering. This is very, very important Kingdom business, Candy."

With the King's words ringing in her ears, Candy started toward Primrose Lane. As she started up the steps to Patty's home, she noticed more changes to the house. Not only were the steps new, but the hand and porch railings as well. In fact, she would declare the shutters had been replaced on the front windows, and that was a new mailbox hanging by the door. Looking around the property, she could see the oak tree had been trimmed, and some of the dead shrubs replaced with fresh green ones. And was that new sod on the side of the lawn? Truly, a transformation was in the making. Yet with the market to tend, a child to care for, and an ailing wife to see after, when had Ken found time to work on the house? She shook her head thoughtfully. Oh well, to the matter at hand.

Entering the home, Candy immediately noticed the absence of Barbara. And was it her imagination, or did the house seem darker today?

"Patty, it's me … Candy. I've come to visit you," she called out.

A disinterested voice replied, "You needn't have bothered. I am not in the mood for visitors today."

With a boldness Candy did not know she was capable of she replied, "That's too bad, because I am here. And we're going to talk."

Caught off guard by Candy's statement, Patty sat up in bed as if she was not sure whether to run, hide, or prepare for a battle.

"What's this I hear about your not coming to the Gathering?" Candy began. "It is ridiculous not to attend. It will be *the* event of the year. Almost the whole town will be there. Everyone has worked so hard to make this a wonderful meeting, and you're not coming!"

Patty would have laughed had Candy not been so serious. She could not help being amused at Candy's outrage over her decision. In fact, in all the years she had known Candy, she had never seen her so adamant about something.

"It's not that I just don't want to come," Patty began to explain. "I really have been planning to come. Lydia and I even discussed what she should wear. But when I began thinking of who would be there, and how long it's been since I have seen most of them …you know, there's no telling what they thought when I left. And then when I abruptly returned ..." her voice trailed off. "The more I thought about it …well, I just could not bring myself to commit to go."

"What on earth are you talking about?" Candy began in her most corrective tone. "Everyone is delighted that you have returned."

"How do you know that?" Patty retorted. "Who has said they are glad I am back?"

In an instant, Candy heard the King's voice, 'Who do you suppose has done the work outside?' Immediately Candy grabbed Patty by the hand. "Come with me! I'll bet you have not been outside this house in days. And I'll bet you have not even seen what has been done."

Practically dragging Patty from the bed, Candy headed toward the door, her reluctant charge in tow. Stepping into the fresh air, where the bright warmth of the morning sun revealed the many improvements, Patty's eyes began to fill with tears.

"You mean others did this for me? At times I heard noises outside, but I just assumed it was Barbara puttering around," Patty cried.

"Not me!" Barbara called, appearing from around the corner. "I don't work outside. I do better inside where it is not so hot. But these young fellows …" she extended her hand in the direction of her helpers,

"They are a different story." At that moment three men emerged, following Barbara to the front of the house — Frank, Hank and Eric, looking like three children caught with their hands in the cookie jar.

"Eric!" Candy shrieked. "What are you doing here? Shouldn't you be at work?"

"Well, I am at work ... sort of. I mean, as leader of the Outreach Council, I thought it would set a good example if I pitched in and helped the fellows who have been working here the past few days."

Eric started up the front steps. "Really Patty, all of us just wanted you to know how happy we are that you've returned to us, and brought your beautiful family." With tears running down her cheeks, all Patty could do was rest her head on Candy's shoulder and sob with disbelief.

"Well, we can stand out here and burn up in this heat or go inside and have a refreshing cup of tea and some of my delicious cookies," Barbara informed the men. Without having to be nudged, they followed her into the house like dutiful schoolboys.

Once inside, the conversation and laughter flowed freely, the years of pain beginning to disappear from Patty's face. And as Barbara hovered over all of them like an old mother hen, it seemed as if even the house took a sigh of relief.

It was at home later that evening when Candy learned how long Eric had been working at Patty's. As it turned out, he had been the one to replace the front steps. And having done that, he realized how many other things needed to be repaired to make the dwelling safe for Lydia. It was then he had spoken to some of the men from the local Gathering, and they agreed it would be a great Kingdom project. In only a few days, much had been accomplished.

-13-

*M*aking her final survey of the King's house and double-checking her list, Candy paused at the sound of the King's voice behind her in the hallway. "That was a great piece of Kingdom business you conducted the other day," he congratulated. "I think Patty was a little in fear of her life for a moment. She said she never knew you had so much spunk in you. In fact, she said if you had spoken like that years ago, she would have been terrified." Both Candy and the King laughed heartily at that thought.

"It was actually your prompting about who had done the work outside that worked the magic, Sir. If you and Eric can so skillfully hide things from me, I will begin to doubt my intuitiveness." The King took her by the hand, and they walked down the hall to the tea room.

"You have no worries in that area. However, I do not tell *all* my citizens the same thing at the same time. On occasion, there are situations which must be kept under wraps until the appropriate time."

"I guess the other afternoon was the appropriate time," Candy laughed.

Sitting down, the King continued. "A lot of good came of that afternoon. Patty is now committed to attending the Gathering. She is still a little hesitant, but she is going to come."

Candy's mind went to another member of the family. "Will Lydia also be attending? I think she would enjoy it so much!"

The King smiled. "Don't worry, my child. The entire family will be front and center."

With those words hid in her heart, Candy completed the inspection of the King's house.

On her way back home, she decided to stop for a chat with her father. Approaching him, Candy thought how much things had changed. There had been a time, many years ago, when she would never have thought she and her father could work together on behalf of the King. In fact, she would never have imagined the two of them doing anything together. Drawing nearer, her father called out to her, "Hello young lady. You certainly look in fine spirits today."

"As do you," she chimed back. "The grounds look lovely, Father. I never realized you had such a green thumb. The shrubs and lawn certainly thrive under your care."

A look of regret briefly crossed his face, "I never gave you much reason to know what I was good at," his voice began to drop.

Candy reached out and gave him a hug. "I love you, Father. That is all we have to remember."

Stooping down to pick up his shovel, Ben asked, "How are my grandchildren? It seems your mother and I never see them enough. Eric dropped by a few days ago to borrow some tools for a project. He looked as fine as ever. He is a good man, Candy."

Candy fairly burst with pride. She was grateful Eric and her father got along well, and Eric was very understanding. He always made sure Ben knew that he was welcome in their home. "We have been so busy with the preparations for the Gathering we have not had time for family visiting, I'm afraid. As soon as things settle down, I want you and Mother to come by for dinner."

Her father gave her a warm smile. "We will look forward to it." Ben understood how hard it had been for Candy to accept and forgive him; and he was grateful for the healing between Candy, his wife, and himself. In fact, he thought as he picked up his tools, some of those roses needed cutting and he knew just the lady to appreciate them. Shirley would certainly enjoy the color and fragrance of these fine specimens.

That evening Shirley did not disappoint Ben. She beamed with the blush of first love at the sight of him making his way up the walk. How he had changed! The man he had once been was now gone. And instead of dreading his homecoming, she looked out the window repeatedly with the hope that he would appear. Waiting for him on the porch, she smiled with delight at his colorful and fragrant offering. As they walked inside arm in arm, she wondered if the neighbors ever considered how different Ben's homecomings were now. A smile covered her face at the thought of how different they truly were.

-14-

$\mathscr{A}$s Ben readied himself for dinner, Shirley announced they were having company drop by for dessert. With a twinkle in his eye he asked, "And who could that possibly be?" His mock question went unanswered, for in the past few years it had become common practice for Barbara and Jack to drop in often, or for Ben and Shirley to visit them. It seemed the two couples had a lot to talk about these days. Victoria and Candy's steadfast friendship had somehow knit the two families together over the years, and they often enjoyed reminiscing together about the many changes in both families as a result of the girls' visits to the tea room.

Later that evening, Barbara and Jack made their way up the familiar steps to the front door. "Well, it is about time you got here," Ben teased. "I was about to help myself to some of this pie."

After hugs all around, the foursome took their usual seats and conversation centered on the topic foremost in everyone's mind. The town was filled with excitement, and each of them had taken part in preparations for the Great Gathering.

"Tell us Barbara," Shirley began. "How are Patty and her family these days?"

Without any coaxing Barbara explained she would soon be out of a job. Patty was gaining strength, and it was only a matter of days until she would be able to care for her family without any help. "I will miss my visits with them," she lamented. "How I will get by without seeing Lydia each day is beyond me. In many ways she reminds me of Victoria when she was young."

"Lydia will be attending the Gathering, won't she?" Ben asked. "I thought I heard that bit of news today while working at the King's house."

"Yes. She will be there with her mother and father," Barbara answered. She hesitated before going on. "I'm not sure why, but Patty seems bothered by something lately. At first I thought she was just nervous about getting reacquainted with people she has not seen in a while, but I think it is more than that. Even when she smiles, there is a touch of sadness that comes through."

"I'm sure she's nervous, Barbara." Jack chimed in. "After all, she knows how folks like to talk. And we all remember what a stir it caused when she disappeared so many years ago. None of us believed her mother's story about her going to live with relatives."

"Yes, it was all quite strange," Shirley agreed. "Wasn't it right after the rebellion was put down that she left? And then just a few weeks later her father passed on. The whole thing is most depressing. Does anyone know where her mother went? At first, we all thought she had joined Patty, yet Patty seemed very surprised not to find her mother here when she returned."

"Yes, it does seem to pose more questions than answers," Ben responded, standing up to pour more tea for everyone.

The folks sitting around Shirley's kitchen table were not the only ones reflecting on Patty and her family that night. Candy had just turned to Eric, voicing a similar question. "Eric, what do you think happened to Patty's mother?"

Eric looked helplessly at her. "I don't know, dear. I guess I've never thought much about it. But I've always believed the shame of what happened with her husband, George, after the rebellion was just too much to bear. I suspect she left out of embarrassment. You recall it was George who led the revolt. He rallied the citizens on that side of town to march against the King and his statutes. In fact, if I remember correctly, he was the one who swung the knife that slashed the King's arm. It was fortunate the blade missed the main artery by a hair's breadth. Otherwise, the King might not be with us."

Candy shuddered at the thought. What would life be like without the King? While she had tried to block the memories of that time from her mind, she recalled the unrest and stress in the city as the King had confronted those in rebellion. He had tried to reason with each of them, showing how the statutes were for their good. But it was to no avail. George had done a thorough job of turning their hearts and minds against the King. And now George was gone, and they were in ruin. And while the King had made several attempts to reconcile with the residents of Primrose Lane, as far as she could tell, it had been useless. The people there seemed determined to live outside the King's statutes. It saddened her heart to think that while they were tenaciously holding on to their possessions (few though they now were), they were missing the joy of experiencing the King's love firsthand. Of course, they enjoyed some Kingdom benefits. Although they did not serve him, the King continued to provide clean water and needed utilities to their homes, and the streets were maintained in good condition. She only wished they could see that living in the Kingdom was more than just having clean water, food, or shelter — it was enjoying a relationship with the King. It was having someone love you just because you were you, not because you were perfect, but because he chose to love you.

-15-

*P*atty's home was filled with activity, and Lydia was bursting with joy at the thought of attending the Gathering. She was not sure what a Gathering was, but anything that caused this much excitement had to be good. "Miss Barbara, are you going to the Gathering," Lydia asked.

"Oh yes, child, I wouldn't miss it for the world."

"I've never been to a Gathering," Lydia explained. "I do hope it is something kids enjoy."

"I don't think you will be disappointed, Lydia," Barbara answered. "Now run along so I can finish my work and get home. I won't be coming so often now that your mother is better. But I must make sure there is plenty of food cooked and stored in the freezer for a few days — just in case your mother needs to rest some before the big day."

Not finding many answers to her questions with Barbara, Lydia decided to ask her mother. "Mom, have you been to the Gathering before?"

With a little hesitancy Patty began, "Not here, Lydia. I attended Gatherings when you were small, but it was in the town we moved from. You know I have not felt well since we arrived, so I haven't attended any here."

"Are they fun?" Lydia quizzed. "You know … like little kid fun? "Patty was amused at how honestly children could express their feelings.

"Are you telling me that unless it is fun, you aren't interested?" Patty laughed.

"Something like that," Lydia confessed.

"But Lydia, there are many types of fun. For example, one kind of fun is where everyone laughs or plays games." She could see Lydia nodding from the corner of her eye. "Then there is the fun that comes from being with people you love and that love you. And sometimes ... just being around certain people can be fun. Do you understand?"

"Sure," Lydia quickly answered. "It's like when Miss Barbara comes to visit. I have fun those days. She doesn't play games or anything, but I sure like it when she is here. Is it like that?"

"You are very perceptive, my dear. It is exactly like that."

Leaning nearer to Patty, she asked, "Will he be there?"

"What 'he' are you referring to, Lydia?"

"You know, the King! Will he be there? I don't think I will like it if he is – even if Miss Barbara and Miss Candy are there."

Patty looked solemnly at her daughter. "What makes you say that, Lydia?"

"Well, it is just that some of the kids on the street say he is very mean. They say if you see him, you should run fast the other way."

"Lydia, I don't know who you have been talking with, but they have not told you the truth. When I was younger, there was a time that I felt the same way these informers of yours feel. But I was wrong, and so are they. He is the kindest man you will ever meet."

"Kinder than Daddy? Kinder than Mr. Eric? Wow, he must be something!"

"Something indeed, my dear. You will see," Patty smiled.

Skipping out the door, Lydia purposed to find out for herself about the King. It might take some doing, but she was sure she could find a way to talk to him. She wanted to know for herself; and if she tried hard, she would surely find out. From talking with the other children, she already knew that he lived across town. That was a long way to go, but it would be worth it. If she just gave it enough thought, she knew she could find a way. It would just take a little planning.

The answer presented itself sooner than Lydia hoped. The next afternoon her father asked if she would like to walk with him to their market. He felt he had left some items out and needed to make sure they were put away properly. Lydia jumped at the chance to walk with her father into the town square. She knew it was only a short distance from the market to the street where the King's house was located. She was very pleased that the answer had come so quickly.

-16-

*A*rriving at the market, Ken realized some of the produce bins had turned over. "Lydia," he began, "it will take me a little while to get this mess cleaned up. Why don't you play in the office while I straighten this out?" And with that suggestion, Lydia's plan came into being. She obediently walked toward the produce office, but when Ken bent over a stack of vegetables, she quickly darted in the opposite direction.

Not really knowing where she was headed, Lydia felt sure she would know the King's house when she saw it. And after turning down a couple of streets without success, she stopped at the sight of a stately structure. Surely that must be the King's house. It was larger than any house on Primrose Lane! In fact, it was the biggest house Lydia had ever seen. Deciding she was at the correct address, she ascended the steps leading to the front door. Though there were a lot of steps for such short legs, she was not deterred. She was going to see for herself what the King was like.

Tugging on the massive wooden doors, Lydia realized they would not budge. Whew! She had never imagined doors could be so heavy. Yet this only assured her that she must be at the correct address; after all, she had heard he was not the sort of person who encouraged visitors. After a couple more tugs at the door handle, Lydia was about to give up in disappointment. She was just stepping away from the doors when one of them opened.

A kindly voice spoke from somewhere above her, "Lydia, were you looking for me?"

Wow! Looking up, Lydia thought he must surely be the tallest man she had ever seen. And now, upon actually seeing him, she was having second thoughts about confronting him.

"Well, Lydia," a smile now covered the tall man's face, "am I who you are looking for?"

Suddenly words began stumbling out of her mouth. "Yes … if you are the King."

"I am certainly the King," he answered. "How may I help you today?"

Pulling up to her full height and with much courage, Lydia responded. "People say you are mean, so I came to find out for myself."

With that, the King could not hold back his laughter any longer. "I must say, Lydia, not many people approach me the first time with as much courage as you. Why don't you come in, and I will try to answer your questions. I was pouring myself some afternoon tea, and I have extra cookies. Would you like to join me?"

The invitation to cookies was more than Lydia could resist. The long walk had made her hungry and thirsty. "I don't mind if I do," she responded in her most grownup voice, but her answer sounded far more confident than she actually was.

Once inside, the King led her to the tea room. And upon walking through the door, Lydia immediately forgot the purpose of her trip. "Wow, how beautiful!"

The King smiled, "Thank you very much, Lydia. Miss Candy and Miss Victoria have always thought so."

At the mention of two of her favorite people, Lydia began to relax. The King placed two cookies on her plate. While deciding how to begin her inquisition, she munched thoughtfully. "These are great chocolate chip cookies — chewy, just the way I like them. How did you know I like chocolate chip? Or is this all you have?"

The King's laughter filled the room. "You sound so much like a little girl I met long ago. She was also surprised to learn that I care enough about the citizens in my Kingdom to know their likes and dislikes."

With the mention of knowing things, Lydia's mind was brought back to her purpose for being there. "That's just the thing," she began. "I am not sure that you really do care about your citizens. In fact, it seems to me that you only want them to do things for you. I don't know of anything you do for them,"

With great concern, the King looked intently at the little girl, his heart broken that one so young could have formed such a harsh opinion of him. "In what ways have I failed to help you, Lydia?" he asked.

A look of consternation crossed her face. Now, being pressed for a particular instance, she was at a loss for one. In truth, she had to admit that her needs were few, and primarily supplied by her mother and father. At the thought of her mother, her face clouded.

"What is bothering you, child?" the King questioned. "It seems there is something heavy on your heart."

"It's just that if you are the King, and kings are supposed to be very powerful, then why does my mother cry a lot?" Lydia fairly shouted.

The King moved closer to the little girl. "Well, sometimes people have disappointments that heal slowly. Or, things happen that people regret. And although they may know there is nothing they can do about it, they still grieve over the situation. Their thoughts often turn to it, and they try to figure out what they could have done differently that might have changed things."

"Like when my mother talks about my grandmother?' Lydia softly responded.

"That's right. Like your grandmother," he kindly comforted.

"You see, Little One ... things were often difficult between your mother and your grandmother. And when your mother returned here, she thought her mother would be here and they could mend much of the hurt between them. But when she arrived, her mother was gone ... and she was very disappointed. She blames herself for not returning sooner."

"Oh ..." was all Lydia could muster.

However, before she could say another word, the large front doors banged open, and Ken could be heard calling out for his daughter. The King rose to meet him. With frustration in each step, Ken approached Lydia.

"Why didn't you stay with me at the market? I turned to speak to you, and you were gone. I looked up and down the market streets, but couldn't find you anywhere. Had it not been for the King's message, I would not have known where you were."

Lydia looked from one man to the other. On one hand, she feared she would be punished for leaving without telling her father; but on the other, she was curious how her father had known where to find her. The King had not left the room since she arrived, so how could he have told anyone?

"I am sorry I worried you. But I was afraid if I told you where I wanted to go, you would never let me come this far. I'm really sorry. But how did the King tell you I was here? He has not left this room since I arrived."

Both Ken and the King smiled at the perplexed look on the child's face. While she knew she had done an awful thing by leaving without permission, she had a look of determination to know how all this had happened.

"Ken, why don't you have a seat?" the King extended a hand. "And I will explain this to Lydia."

"Child," he turned to face Lydia again, "I know you have mixed feelings about me, but your father does not. Your father trusts me completely. And when I have such a relationship with someone, my heart has the ability to speak to their heart no matter where they are. I knew your father would be concerned about you, so I spoke to his heart … telling him you were with me, and that he was not to worry. I told him to come and walk you home."

Lydia looked into her father's eyes, "Is that true, Father? Can you hear the King's heart speak to you?"

Ken took Lydia on his lap, wrapping his arms around her. It was good to know she was safe. "Yes Lydia, the King and I have been friends for a long time. In fact, I was not much older than you when I first met him."

"Did mother meet him a long time ago?' Lydia searched her father's face for answers.

"In a way. She was older than you when she came to the place of needing his friendship."

"So mother is his friend also? But …" Lydia's heart was still not at peace. "If she is his friend, why doesn't he help her? A king can do anything. Mother is sad, and I want her to be happy."

Ken looked at the King questioningly, so the King spoke softly to Lydia. "Child, your mother will be happy again soon. Sometimes things happen in people's lives that take a little while to work out — even for a King. Trust me, Lydia. I love you, your mother, and your father very much. I work constantly to make things good for you. I am always thinking of you, and trying to sort out things so that you can have peace and joy. But sometimes people make bad choices, and it is not always easy to set things right. But I will not fail you, Lydia. Trust me. Let me work on your behalf. You will not be disappointed, I promise. But some things take time ..."

Looking deeply into the King's eyes, Lydia knew he spoke the truth. And while she did not have all the answers she came for, she realized that she was leaving with something she had not expected — a growing affection for the King. With this much resolved, Ken and Lydia started for home.

Watching them go down the steps, the King knew that his plans would have to be stepped up. After all, the day of the Gathering was drawing near; and the answers to Lydia's questions were a big part of that day. He must not … he would not … fail her!

-17-

"I thought you two would have been back long ago. After all, how long does it take to straighten a few produce bins?" Patty asked, as Ken and Lydia came through the door.

Lydia looked up questioningly at her father. Winking in her direction, Ken answered, "There's nothing wrong with a father dragging something out a little longer to spend extra time with his daughter, is there?"

Patty smiled, giving them both a big hug. How happy she was that Lydia had a father who loved her and was not afraid to let that love show. But as that thought came to her mind, other thoughts from long ago also presented themselves, and a hint of fear crossed her face. Watching his wife closely, Ken did not miss the expression. "Patty, what did Barbara leave us for supper tonight?" he asked, diverting her attention.

Shaking off the dark feeling, Patty flashed back, "I'll have you know that I prepared tonight's meal for you. After all, I am much stronger now and it is time I took care of my family myself."

With that said, she led the way to the dining table which had been set with their best china. Lovely green salads were already placed at each setting. Ken made a grand gesture of seating each of his ladies at the table. With a festive mood in the air, they bantered back and forth over dinner, each one sharing interesting tidbits from the events of the day. Lydia's visit with the King, however, remained a special secret between father and daughter. Watching her father as they finished the evening meal, Lydia knew she had the best father ever. No one had a father as handsome or strong or wonderful as she.

Finally, with Lydia put to bed and the kitchen cleaned up from the evening meal, Ken and Patty took a moment to talk. "You seemed troubled this evening." Ken tentatively inquired. "Is everything alright?"

"You're very perceptive," Patty nodded. "It's just that when you were talking about how much you enjoy spending time with Lydia, I was thinking of my father. I have no memory of his ever taking time out of his day for me, and I really missed that. You and your father have wonderful conversations when you are together, and both of you speak of the great times you had when you were growing up. Not everyone has such memories. I wonder if you realize how special that is."

Ken carefully considered his answer, "You're right, Patty. He is my best friend, and those are treasured times. I make a special effort to let my father know how much I appreciate all he's done for me." He smiled thoughtfully, "I do hope they will be able to attend the Gathering … and bring Carol also."

At the mention of her friend's name, Patty's heart warmed with loving memories. It was Carol who had given her a job after she left here so many years ago. It was Carol who had taken her to the Gathering that first time. And in a way, she even had Carol to thank for her wonderful husband, because she had introduced them. She owed Carol a great deal.

"I've made the extra bedrooms ready for them. I certainly hope they are able to come," Patty agreed. "It would be wonderful to see them again. Since my father passed away and I can't locate my mother, Carol is the closest thing to family that I have — except for you and Lydia, of course."

It was getting late, so they reluctantly said their goodnights and began to settle into bed. And while sleep came easily that night for Ken, Patty lay awake, struggling with her feelings. She was grateful for Carol in her life, but how wonderful it would be to have her own mother with her. 'Well, you can't un-spill milk,' she reminded herself, finally drifting off. 'You must learn to be grateful for what you have.'

The next day dawned clear and bright. Soon after lunch, Patty heard voices on the front lawn. Looking out the window, she saw them — all three of them! Laughing, Rex, Betty, and Carol trudged up the sidewalk, luggage in hand. "Oh my, let me help you with those!" Patty laughed, flying down the front steps in excitement.

"Now, now," Rex cautioned, "we are managing just fine. You know you should not exert yourself. We want you strong for the big day!"

The little group made their way into the house amid much joking and laughter. And after getting settled in their rooms, everyone gathered for tea on the front porch. Relaxed and comfortable, someone mentioned how nice everything looked. Patty admitted this had not been the case just a few days earlier. She explained that with Ken working long hours and her not as well as she had hoped, members of the Kingdom had joined in, putting things in good order.

"That's just the sort of thing I've come to expect from citizens who live according to Kingdom Statutes," Carol beamed. Rex and Betty agreed, adding that on many occasions they had been called upon to lend their talents and resources to help others.

"What time will Lydia be home from day school?" Betty wanted to know, trying to contain her anticipation. "And Ken? When does he usually arrive?"

"Not long," Patty assured her, realizing it had been a long while since her mother-in-law had seen her son and granddaughter.

The afternoon flew past, punctuated by the sound of tea cups clinking on saucers and the easy flow of loving conversation between Patty and her guests. And before any of them realized it, Ken was coming up the walk, with Lydia in hand. As everyone stood to greet the duo, Lydia bounced up the steps — the first recipient of hugs and kisses — making her rounds through the little group.

Surveying her son's face, Betty was happy to see that while things had been difficult, Ken seemed to be holding up just fine. Before she could move in closer, however, Rex grabbed Ken in a bear hug declaring how wonderful it was to see him again.

After a brief catching up, Patty announced she was going to the kitchen to see what could be prepared for dinner. After all, with Barbara no longer coming everyday, it was up to the lady of the house to prepare a meal for the guests. Assuring her that they had come to 'serve' and not 'be served', the two ladies joined her in the kitchen, their domestic chatter enhancing the preparation of the evening meal. Lydia, however, accompanied her father and grandfather to the living room.

-18-

Making her way about the kitchen, Candy could hardly contain herself. It was finally here! Only a few hours from now they would all make their way to the King's house for the Gathering. But as she stood at the refrigerator contemplating what to prepare for breakfast, her thoughts were interrupted by a loud knock on the back door and the excited twitter of female voices outside.

Flinging open her kitchen door, Candy's mouth fell open at the sight of Sarah, Kathryn, and Susan, looking as pleased to see her as she was shocked at seeing them. Smiling broadly, their arms filled with baskets of fruit, breads and jams, they entered the kitchen in a bustle of activity.

"What on earth are you doing here at this time of day?" Candy teased.

"We were talking last night ... remembering how shocked you were all those years ago when Victoria invited us to tea without telling you ..." Susan began.

"And we thought you were due for another surprise ..." Kathryn chimed in, picking up the story.

"So here we are!" Sarah concluded, with laughter. "We came to have morning tea with you!"

Though early morning would not have been Candy's choice of meeting time, she was nonetheless pleased to be reunited with her friends of long ago. The girls made themselves at home, setting out silverware and plates, and arranging the pastries, fruit, jams and breads on the dining table. Putting on the kettle for tea, Candy joined them, her own voice rising and falling with theirs. It was good to be together again. Suddenly, it was as if her little kitchen was bursting with conversation and laughter.

There was so much to share that it seemed they were all talking at once.

With such commotion going on in the kitchen, there was little hope of reading the morning newspaper. Putting it aside and following the sound of laughter, Eric came upon the four women sitting around the dining table laughing, talking, and joking like children of long ago. His gaze resting on his wife, he smiled to himself, his heart filled with love. It was good to see her so relaxed and at peace. Such a treasure she was to him — always there to encourage, lifting his spirits when he was down. And she was a wonderful mother to his children, not to mention being one of the main strengths of the community. Yes, he was indeed a blessed man. Life could not have been any better.

"Well, I see this is no place for a man today," he laughed, making his way toward Candy.

"Oh, Eric, you remember Susan, Sarah, and Kathryn don't you?" Candy said, getting up to pour Eric's morning tea.

"How could I ever forget them?" Eric teased. "They were my greatest competitors for your time, if I remember correctly."

The women laughed, retorting they'd only been looking out for Candy's 'best interest' and it was 'for her own good' that they'd limited the amount of time she had to spend with him all those years ago in high school. He took their jibes in good-natured fun. Finally, their camaraderie reaching new heights, Eric retreated, saying he would take the children to breakfast at the local diner, lest they interrupt the 'reunion of the century'.

With Candy's blessing, Eric and the children headed out, promising to join her at the Gathering later in the day. Before they knew it, the morning flew by as if it had wings. It was getting late. So with assurances of family pictures to be shared and addresses exchanged, they hugged each other and parted company, everyone hurrying toward the long awaited event.

Yet the three friends had scarcely cleared the sidewalk until there was another knock on Candy's door. Thinking one of her friends had forgotten something, Candy pulled open the door to be surprised for the second time that day. On the other side of the door stood Victoria. But she was not alone.

Candy studied her visitors. For a moment, the woman with Victoria seemed somehow familiar, but her face was not one she could recall.

"May we come in Candy? We need your help with a matter … it is important Kingdom Business."

Candy nodded in agreement, and Victoria and the woman made their way to the table and sat down. "Candy, do you remember Linda?" Seeing her confusion, Victoria hastily added, "Patty's mother?"

Trying not to look as shocked as she felt, Candy replied, "Of course I do. How lovely to see you again." Linda did not respond immediately to Candy's words, so Victoria went on.

"I am sure you know about many of the things concerning Patty and her family."

Candy solemnly nodded.

"Linda and I have been visiting for several weeks now," Victoria began. "Like you and I, Linda also had many issues to work through. Based on what we heard as children and the things we all imagined later, I'm sure you can appreciate how being here in this city is quite difficult for her. But, as we have talked these past weeks, she has realized that avoiding things does not make them go away ... in fact, it only postpones what must be faced sooner or later."

Looking in Linda's direction, Candy could see tears beginning to fill her eyes. Her heart went out to the woman; and reaching over, she put her arms around her in a loving embrace. Suddenly, Linda could no longer hold back her tears; and burying her face in Candy's shoulder, she sobbed like a frightened child. And as Candy comforted her, allowing her to cry, Victoria began to explain why she was with her. "Linda is willing to attend the Gathering today."

Trying not to betray her own belief that this was really not a good idea, Candy murmured, "Oh really? How nice."

Victoria turned toward Candy, her look penetrating. "We have been friends too long for you to try and your hide feelings from me," she chided. "I know you feel this is not a good idea. But the King and I have discussed it, and we feel it is the best course of action."

At the mention of the King's input, Candy began to relax somewhat, but she said nothing.

Victoria went on. "Candy, do you recall how the King taught us that often in Kingdom business what affects one person has an impact on others?"

Candy nodded.

"Today's events can influence all of the citizens in our city. Wounds which have long festered in the hearts of many can be healed. Linda is willing to do her part, and I need you to make sure Patty does hers."

Puzzled, Candy looked up. "Does Patty know her mother is here?"

"No, she does not. The King and I felt it would be better if they met each other on neutral ground ... at the King's house. There has been so much pain and disappointment in their family that we believe this reunion must be done in an atmosphere of love and acceptance."

"What do you need me to do?" Candy asked hesitantly.

"Just make sure Patty is at the Gathering. In her heart, she is still nervous about seeing everyone. She is uncertain how she will be received. She still does not realize how much she is loved."

Relieved that her part was only to ensure that Patty arrived, Candy quickly agreed to get dressed and make her way to Patty's house. Since Eric and the children were already gone, it would not be a problem. "But I am not to mention Linda to Patty at all?" Candy confirmed.

Victoria nodded, as she and Linda prepared to leave. "That's right. Just make sure Patty is at the Gathering. The King and I will handle the rest."

-19-

*C*andy's mind was in a whirl as she made her way down Primrose Lane. She wondered … how would she have felt if she'd not seen her own father in many years? And then, he suddenly appeared out of the blue? It was a stressful thought, and she was unsure how she would have handled such a situation. She sighed heavily, considering how this all might end. Undoubtedly, it could ruin the Gathering. 'Why couldn't Linda have returned sooner?' she thought to herself, hurrying her pace. They had spent so many weeks in preparation, and everyone had worked so hard to make things perfect

… and now, to have a shadow cast over the big event by this untimely reunion. 'If Linda had wanted to see her daughter, she could have found her before now,' she thought to herself. 'Or if Patty was unsure whether her mother was alive or dead, she should have looked for her!' This was certainly turning out to be a very stressful day.

As she approached the door, it opened with a frantic Ken standing behind it. "I'm so glad you're here," he said breathlessly. "It's Patty. She says she simply cannot go with Lydia and me to the Gathering today. I told her that Carol and my Mom and Dad were expecting her to attend, but it didn't make any difference. She just sits and cries. She says she cannot face everyone."

Candy brushed by Ken with hardly a word. In her heart, she could hear the King say, 'the Kingdom is counting on you'. True to Ken's description, there sat Patty, her eyes swollen and red from crying. As she looked up and saw Candy, it was if all strength left her.

"Don't even start, Candy. I can't do it. I don't feel well. It is too much to expect from me. I just cannot go."

Knowing what was awaiting Patty at the Gathering, Candy almost wanted to agree, and assure her she did not have to attend. But that would never do. She had her instructions and she would be faithful to execute them.

Candy's voice was firm, and her tone unbending. "I am here to *take* you to the Gathering, Patty. I am *not* here to *ask* you to come."

The look in Candy's eyes made Patty rethink her strategy. She'd seen that look before; and she knew it would be hard, if not impossible, to dissuade her.

"I know the King sent you," she began, her voice pleading. "But if he really loves me, he will understand. If he will give me more time, I know I will be able to come next year. In fact, I will promise to make every effort to attend the small weekly Gatherings. Really … I'm just not up to this right now."

"This is not up to you, Patty," Candy replied, her voice raised and stern. "This is about the Kingdom. At times, we all must do things we don't want to do or think we can't do. Yet we find the strength to do them. We do what we know is good for the Kingdom. This is such a day. If you do not come today, you will regret it the rest of your life."

Just then they heard a deep sigh coming from the doorway, followed by Lydia's small voice. "Mother, if you don't go, then I won't go. I know you don't want to go because the King is really *not* a kind person."

Patty held out her arms. "Child, why do you say that? He is wonderful and loving and kind. He has done so much for me … and for you and your father as well."

"I've only met him once, and I guess he was nice enough," Lydia began. "But if you have known him a long time and don't want to go to his house, you must know something about him that you're not telling me."

Candy looked knowingly at Patty, as if to say, 'How are you going to straighten out this mess?'

Drawing the child closer, Patty spoke again. "Long ago I lived in this house as a little girl like you. But unlike ours, my family was not a happy one.

My father was not kind and loving like your father. My mother was sad all the time, and my father was angry about almost everything. There came a time when I could not stay here any longer, so I ran away. I thought that was the only way I could settle things in my mind and heart."

At this news, Lydia's eyes got big and her mouth fell open. The thought of her mother doing something so wrong was startling. Then she remembered that she too had recently needed to find answers to some of her questions … and had left without telling anyone.

"Lydia, it was the King who made sure I found a good home with Aunt Carol. It was the King who made it possible for me to meet your daddy. It was the King who made it possible for us to move here. He knew I hoped to find my mother … but I waited too long. He has been kinder to me than you can possibly imagine."

"But if he has been so kind, why won't you go to his house?" said Lydia with the wisdom of the ages.

"Why not, indeed?" chimed in Rex, Betty, Carol, and Ken, who had quietly entered, and waited by the door. Looking from person to person, Patty was thankful for the love she saw in their eyes.

Crossing the room, Ken knelt beside his wife. "Sweetheart, come with us. We will surround you. What do you have to fear? What does it matter if a few people who don't understand whisper? You will be there with people who love you, and you will be there to honor the King who has done so much for us."

"Okay," she sighed, unable to resist. "Now, out you all go while I get dressed. Candy … can you stay and help me get ready?'

-20-

*P*roceeding toward the King's house, the little group kept the conversation constant and lighthearted, sensing it was crucial to keep Patty's mind off what lay behind the massive wooden doors of the King's house. And though Candy alone knew the revelation that awaited Patty, there was a sense that each of them was about to become part of something very important.

At the bottom of the steps Patty hesitated, a sense of fear evident in her eyes. Putting her arm around her, Candy whispered, "Did you know that Victoria once hesitated in this exact spot? She too debated about whether to go up these steps. Think what we would have missed," she smiled, "had she not gone in." And with that admonition ringing in her ears, Patty pushed ahead, her family and Candy encircling her.

Near the top of the steps they found Eric, Brett and Karen. "We decided to wait out here for you, so we could all walk in together," Eric greeted them. Patty seemed relieved to have more support accompany her entrance. Once inside, however, she started to indicate they should take seats near the back. But Candy would have no part of that!

"No you don't, my friend. You and your family are going to sit with me and my family ... right up front." And before Patty could protest, Candy had propelled her down the aisle and into the third row of seats.

Sitting down between Candy and Ken, Patty felt sure she could hear muffled whispers. Surely they must be talking about her. It took all her strength to resist the urge to get up and run away. But just as she was considering the possibility of making such an exit, the King came into the room.

Watching him enter, the people stood and began singing the songs of the Kingdom. Afterward, the King began speaking about some of the principles of the Kingdom. He reminded them that each person had problems to be overcome; and explained that living in the Kingdom did not mean things went smoothly all the time, or that every person was always perfect. He emphasized that everyone needed to be forgiven on occasion, and that each citizen must help others find the way of fuller obedience to Kingdom statutes so that all might walk in peace and joy. As he continued teaching, the King explained that every citizen failed to observe Kingdom principles at times. Yet as they became aware of these violations and felt genuine sorrow for their actions, he extended forgiveness to them. He said it was crucial to put yourself in another's position; and that by doing so, it was easier to forgive whatever they might have done that offended or hurt you.

Just as the King was about to make another point in his teaching, a stir began toward the back of the room. Whispered voices rose, becoming louder. Everyone turned to see what was causing the disturbance. Candy reached out to steady Patty, noting that all color had drained from her face. Coming down the aisle was Victoria, and beside her walked Linda. A shocked murmur passed through the room. Half of those present whispered in disbelief of what they were seeing while the others sat like statues in stunned silence. The King stopped speaking and looked toward Victoria.

"I am so glad you ladies were able to join us today," the King said as if Linda's presence was a common occurrence. Finishing his sentence, he looked at Patty, sitting as if she were frozen.

"What is it mother? What's wrong?"

"It's alright Lydia," Ken calmed her. "It's just that your mother was not expecting Miss Victoria and her friend to be here today."

As Victoria took her seat, Linda went and stood beside the King. Her head down, she still looked badly shaken.

"Patty," the King invited, "will you join us?"

At first, Patty could not move a muscle. Then, as if she was a child once again, she ran toward her mother. "Mother, is it really you? I can't believe this! I thought something had happened to you ..."

Her face a palette of emotions, Patty's words began to pour forth as though a dam had burst. Suddenly everything she had longed to ask or share in the years that had been lost to her began to tumble out. "I expected you to be here when I came back, but you weren't ... Why weren't you? Mother, where have you been? I'm so sorry I left so abruptly. I know you worried. But I came back so you would know I was alright, and ... I'm married now! And ... Look mother ... I have a daughter! Lydia? Come here! I want you to meet your grandmother."

Lydia turned to her father, her expression questioning. She had not seen her mother like this before. And she had never seen her grandmother.

Ken reached for Lydia's hand. "Come on," he said. "I'll go with you." Taking it, Lydia was grateful to have her father's strong hand over her own and for his steady presence beside her.

As Ken and Lydia drew near, Linda turned to face her small granddaughter. Suddenly, her reserve of emotion finally unleashed, she reached out to her. Lydia, suddenly overcome with uncharacter-istic shyness, remained slightly behind her father, not sure what to do.

In a gesture of reassurance to Lydia and her grandmother, Ken reached out and embraced Linda. "I'm glad to finally meet you," he said. "I've looked forward to this day for a long time." Turning back to his daughter, his voice was reassuring. "It's alright, Lydia. Don't you want to say 'Hello' to your grand-mother? I'm sure she has been eager to meet you."

With great hesitancy, Lydia stepped from behind her father and moved a little closer to Linda. "Is it true? Have you really been waiting to meet me? If you wanted to meet me, why didn't you come find me?" Lydia asked in her usual forthright manner. Patty intercepted the question for Linda.

"We can talk about that later," she told her daughter. "The important thing now is that we are all together."

With *all* of her family finally near her, Patty's heart overflowed. Turning to the King, she expressed her feelings of love to him. "Sir, you made all this possible. How can I ever thank you?" Her eyes downcast, she then began to speak of other things too long left unspoken.

"Even though you did so much for me … like placing me in Carol's home, a part of me was still angry with you. Somehow I felt you could have done more. I didn't understand why my mother wasn't waiting for me when I returned. I always felt you knew where she was, but were unwilling to tell me."

"Patty, I have always known you felt that way," the King explained. "But even in my Kingdom, things are not always quickly or easily remedied. You wanted Linda to come back, but Linda wasn't sure that she wanted to come back. Yes, she longed to see you … but there are many memories here for her … and not many of them are good. She was not sure she had the strength to endure what might await her."

Hearing the King's words, it was as if suddenly Linda found herself. And turning to those gathered, she began to speak. "Most of you know who I am. And those of you who do not know me personally certainly know of the trouble brought upon the city during the rebellion. I am here to tell you how sorry I am for my part in all of it. While it is true that it was my husband who lead the rebellion, I could have stood up for what was right … but I was weak. I kept quiet, hoping things would work out. That was wrong. I know now that when people know what is right and don't do it, things rarely work out right. I should have made a stand then, but I didn't. But I'm here now … and I am not running from my responsibilities any longer. I ask forgiveness of any one here who was harmed during that horrible time. I have spent many months — years actually — speaking with the King about that time, and he has forgiven me for what I did, as well as what I failed to do. He has spoken truth to me from the Kingdom statutes and principles and has mended my heart, and I have made the decision to no longer live in the shadow of my past mistakes. I have a daughter, a granddaughter, and a son-in-law, and they deserve to have a completed family. There is nothing I can do about the past, but I intend to shape the future according to the King's statutes. All I ask is that you give me a chance."

As Linda finished speaking, people began to rise to their feet. Loud applause broke out from every corner of the auditorium. Immediately, a line began to form, with Barbara and Jack leading the way. Each person at the Gathering embraced Linda and spoke their forgiveness to her. As Linda and her little family made their way back to their seats, the King took the platform.

"What happened here today," he said with a smile, "is a good example of Kingdom principles in action." The King spent the remainder of the time explaining to his citizens the great power of what they had seen. He encouraged everyone to search their hearts, making sure that no one felt forgiveness was being withheld from them. Their free dispersal of forgiveness, he explained, could change even the hardest of hearts. Following the King's teaching, there was more singing of the songs of the Kingdom. Afterward, everyone moved to the tea room where Candy had prepared refreshments for everyone.

As the people gathered in the tea room, Victoria and Candy acted as hostesses. Having the room once again filled with love and laughter reminded them of days spent here many years ago. The King came and stood with them.

"It is amazing what happens when people choose to live according to the Kingdom Statutes," he smiled. "And it especially pleases me when they realize that these statutes were written for *their* good. It is my greatest desire that all of my citizens live in joy and peace."

Candy and Victoria nodded, agreeing that this was surely the way things were meant to be. The day passed swiftly; and after much conversation and numerous pots of tea, the crowd began to disperse, slowly making their way back toward their homes. As Victoria and Candy washed and put away the last of the tea sets, the King lingered to visit Patty and her family and guests, who were among the last to leave.

"It would seem your family has enlarged today," the King said as they parted.

"Yes," Patty beamed in reply. "Carol, Mother, and I have a lot of catching up to do."

"Don't forget about me," Lydia chimed in.

"How could anyone ever forget you, Lydia?" said the King with a wink, leaning over to give her a hug.

Surrendering to his embrace, she wrapped her arms around his neck and whispered, "You really are as nice as Miss Victoria said. You do love us, and want us to be happy. Thank you for bringing my grandmother home."

As Candy headed home to Eric and her children, Victoria decided this might be a good time to visit her own mother and father. Gathering her things, she started out; then paused. Perhaps she should see if the King had further instructions. She found him looking thoughtfully out the window.

"Things went well today, don't you think?" she began.

Turning to face her, the King smiled. "Yes, they did. Thank you, Victoria. Once again, the Kingdom has been blessed because of your obedience."

"It is no burden to obey your instructions, Sir. I understand that it is your heart-felt desire to bring joy and peace to us. And it is my pleasure to do what you ask of me." Once again, she turned toward the door. "I will be going now if you have no further need of me today. I thought this might be a good time to visit my parents."

"An excellent idea," the King agreed. "You run along now. We will soon know what will come of today's activities … and the next step that must be taken. Be ready for anything – and at all times, Victoria. I may call at any moment."

-21-

*T*hrilled to once again be near her family, Linda found herself especially happy to become better acquainted with her new granddaughter. It warmed her heart to watch Lydia at play, her antics often reminding her of Patty as a child. One thing she especially enjoyed was walking Lydia to school each morning.

"It will be a good time for the two of us to become better acquainted," she told Patty. "We need to make up for the time we've lost."

Secretly, she also hoped to renew acquaintance with many who had once been her friends and neighbors on Primrose Lane. And her morning walk with Lydia would offer an excellent opportunity to do so. Like her, the neighborhood had suffered difficult times. But when the King helped her find the courage to return, Linda's heart had become light and free. Now she longed to share her happiness with everyone, confident that happier times also awaited her old neighborhood. Unfortunately, however, not everyone was pleased.

Walking Lydia to school, Linda always smiled, offering a hearty 'Good Morning' to everyone they met. Yet it seemed that no one ever smiled back, or acknowledged her greeting. And when she called them by name, they only stared at her. In fact, they often made rude comments or muttered grumpily to themselves. "They're just having a bad day," she told Lydia as they hurried on, but inwardly a deep sense of foreboding was growing.

Yet one morning when the people coming toward her crossed to the other side of the street, Linda realized her former neighbors were avoiding her, and she decided to speak to Victoria about it.

"I'm having difficulty settling back into my neighborhood," she confided that afternoon over a cup of mint tea. "It seems no matter how hard I try to engage people in conversation, it is fruitless. They ignore me, make ugly comments, or scowl at me. I'm really troubled by this. What do you think is wrong?" Victoria stared into her tea cup, her brow furrowed. Over the past few years, she and Linda had become good friends. She had visited her often in another city before she had returned. It was during these visits she had encouraged Linda to return home, promising her support for the day of the Gathering. Along with Candy, she had worked diligently to ensure Patty attended the Gathering.

Now she looked up at her friend, her face somber. She could see how hard Linda was trying, and knew how painful it was for her to be treated so hatefully. Though she longed to comfort her, how could she tell her what lay at the base of her neighbors' reactions? Victoria sighed, setting her teacup down. No, she was not the one to address this issue. This was a matter for the King.

"Linda," she finally spoke, her voice was husky. "The King is currently present with us. Why don't you visit with him concerning this matter? I believe he will have the answers you seek."

Linda nodded wordlessly. She knew that was the best course of action, and purposed in her heart to visit the King the following day after she walked Lydia to school.

———————

Waving good-bye to her granddaughter, Linda turned down the street toward the King's house early the next morning. The sky was clear and bright. It was a wonderful day for a walk. Yet after only a few steps, she noticed her palms were cold and sweating.

'Why am I so nervous?' she wondered to herself. 'After all, it's not the first time I've met with the King'. Nevertheless, there was a vague sense of foreboding in her heart that she did not understand. Could it be there was more to this matter than she yet realized? Yes … there was an uneasy sense about all of this. Victoria had sensed it too, of that she was certain. She and Victoria had become very close, and they could talk about anything. Yet she had suggested this was a matter to be discussed with the King. That meant this matter was different from anything Victoria had previously encountered. Linda sighed heavily, her heart filled with a strange uneasiness. Slowly she mounted the steps leading to the front door. But before she could pull on the door handle, the big wooden door opened.

"Come in, Linda," the King smiled, compassion in his eyes. "I've been expecting you."

The King's own heart was heavy because of the sadness he saw etched in her face. If only this could have been avoided. Why did the citizens continue to think they knew what was best for the Kingdom? He wanted only abundant life for everyone in his Kingdom. At this moment, however, there was one resident of the Kingdom weighted down with care, and she needed his attention.

The aroma of freshly brewed tea wafted through the air as the King led the way into the tea room. Linda smiled, though somewhat nervously, and took her seat. Watching him preparing the tea, she remembered how many times the comfort of his kind words and a warm cup of tea had set her heart at ease.

"I know you have a lot on your mind," his tone was soft and inviting. "Would you like to tell me about it?"

"Starting will be difficult, Sir," she whispered. "I don't know what I expected exactly, but I can tell you this ... the way people are acting is not it. I have tried to visit my former neighbors, but they pretend not to be home or give me a curt dismissal when they answer the door. I wanted to re-establish relationships with them. I wanted to explain why I felt I had to leave. Most of all, I wanted to apologize for George's deception in leading them away from the Kingdom. But it seems I will not be able to do this. I can't reach them. I don't have the words they are willing to hear. Perhaps I should plan to leave soon. Patty and her family are doing fine, and there is no real need for me to stay here."

The King looked away, his voice thoughtful when he spoke. "No real need for you to be here? Are you sure that is a correct assessment of things ... or just your pain speaking? It would seem to me that Patty, Ken and Lydia need you very much. It has been years since Patty has smiled so freely. A load has been lifted from Ken's shoulders just knowing you are here to help care for Patty, and attend to Lydia. And Lydia ... well, how would you explain to her that the grandmother she has just found suddenly feels the need to leave her? No, I don't think you are reasoning properly. I think you are reacting to the rejection of your neighbors."

Linda looked down at her feet. He was right. And her heart was breaking at the thought. It would be almost unbearable to leave Patty and Lydia now. Yet how could she handle the rejection that constantly confronted her?

"Linda, it will take more than just you to set this thing right. Though you are unaware of it, many who attended the recent Gathering have been talking with me about unity. Having witnessed your reunion with Patty and observing how quickly you forgave each other, they now desire a healing of the division within the Kingdom. Many have purposed in their hearts to find a way to show the residents of Primrose Lane that they are loved. They want everyone to once again be a part of the community, and bring an end to the pain that has hovered over that area so long."

Linda's face lit up. If others joined her in the restoration of her neighborhood, there was hope. And she was ready for whatever project lay ahead.

"We are having a meeting this evening. Bring your family. Let's put all our thoughts together. I know we can arrive at the perfect solution. I have wanted to do this for a long time, but first it was necessary that all of you become willing to set aside your feelings and do what is best for the Kingdom."

"I'll stop by the market and tell Ken," Linda offered. "Then I'll prepare supper and get Patty and Lydia ready. We will be here. You can count on it."

Walking her to the door, the King thought of all she had been through. Life had surely not been easy for her. He was grateful she had agreed to remain in the city. Given time, he knew her little family would experience a future filled with great joy. But often it took a while to sort things out … even for a King.

-22-

$\mathcal{A}$s the King approached the Gathering room, he could hear the hum of conversation. It seemed that although the reason for the meeting was serious, the people were in a positive mood. Entering, he walked toward the front of the room. Quickly people became quiet, intent on hearing what he had to say. Looking around, the King's heart was filled with love for the people gathered before him. Their love and devotion to him and his Kingdom was evident, and he understood that it was not always easy for them to adhere to Kingdom statutes. After all, it was human nature to want your own way. Yet each one present had put aside personal desires time and again, and made the Kingdom first in their hearts. He regretted having to call upon their generosity again; but He knew each person understood the power of love, and He knew they would step forward again.

"I am glad to see all of you tonight," he began. "I know each of you is busy, and there are many demands for your time. It warms my heart to know you are willing to help any way you can."

A man at the back rose, his hat in his hands. "I am so grateful for all you have done for me that … I had to come," he said. Others murmured agreement.

"Thank you, Ben," the King acknowledged him.

Shirley, Ben's wife, reached over and took his hand, beaming with pride at her husband. Truly, their family did have much to be grateful for — and it was all because of the King.

"The time has come to do something about Primrose Lane," the King announced.

A hush fell over the room. People looked at each other, unspoken questions on every face. Everyone knew how patient the King had been with the residents of Primrose Lane. Had the time finally come when he would no longer tolerate their behavior? Would he have them expelled from their homes?

"Before any of you let your imaginations run wild," the King's voice was firm. "I want to publicly declare my love for each resident of Primrose Lane. In fact, it is my love for them that has initiated this meeting. I love them so much that I cannot continue to let them destroy themselves. So ..." the King stepped down from the podium and began walking among the people, "I am going to launch a program designed to show them how much I love them, and how much every member of the Kingdom loves them. We will shower them with unconditional love in a measure they have never seen before. Then, if they decide to live outside Kingdom influence, I will leave them to their choice."

"I feel I must make this attempt," the King went on. "I have watched as they have ignored Linda these past few weeks. And I have heard the cruel remarks they make when they think no one can hear. The time has come to settle this."

The gravity of the King's words was evident, and the people waited in silence. It was not often they saw him so serious. Usually, it was the citizens whose hearts were heavy, and his was the voice of encouragement. Yet now, they felt as though they should encourage him.

Jack spoke the feelings of the group. "You can count on us for anything you need done, Sir."

With great love, the King looked first at Jack, then at the others seated around the room. "I knew that I could," he said. "Let's get started."

Opening a city map, the king indicated the location of each neighborhood. Many of those gathered were surprised to see that Primrose Lane was almost in the exact center of the city.

"Now do you see why it is so important to bring this neighborhood back into fellowship with the rest of the city?" the King asked. "By virtue of its location, it represents the very *heart* of the city. And unfortunately for us, the heart of this city is ill. But I have a plan to correct that." He smiled broadly, his voice filled with enthusiasm, "We are going to rebuild Primrose Lane!"

A collective gasp could be heard in the room. People looked around at each other, surprise and shock written on their faces. Finally, Ben spoke, his voice a little shaky. "We're going to do what?"

"You heard correctly," said the King. "We are going to put the neighborhood back just as it was before the rebellion. Every house will be painted, every broken step repaired, every dead shrub replanted, and every lawn replaced with new sod. And it shall be done as a gift. They are not to pay for anything, and we shall not allow them to help. In fact, it must happen almost without them knowing we are there."

Silence filled the room. Somewhat surprised, the King looked from person to person, searching each pair of eyes for a response. Finally, Candy rose to her feet. "Sir, you spoke on the day of the Great Gathering about forgiveness. You challenged each of us to forgive any wrong done to us. I feel that we each have tried to do that since you spoke. I know that I personally tried to think of things in my past for which I still held resentment … and I made a commitment to free the people who had caused me harm. Surely it is enough to forgive someone in your heart. In my heart, I have committed to love and forgive the residents of Primrose Lane. Isn't that enough?"

"That's a good point, Candy," the King responded. "But let me ask you something. If you have forgiven people on Primrose Lane for any hurt they caused you, how will they know you have done that?"

Suddenly revelation began to dawn in Candy's thinking. Certainly there were times when action spoke louder than words. Sometimes people only believed what they saw, not what they heard. "I see your point, Sir," she said. "What is your plan to make this forgiveness a reality to the residents of Primrose Lane?"

With eyes shining with approval, the King laid out his plan. Each resident of Primrose Lane would receive notice to evacuate for a major overhaul of municipal facilities, and prepare to be away for forty-eight hours. That should allow plenty of time for the necessary revamping of the street.

He then set about making assignments and listing the supplies needed for each work project. Before long, all hesitancy concerning the project had faded from the room. Because the King's excitement was contagious, it was impossible for anyone to withhold whole-hearted approval.

-23-

$\mathscr{A}$mid much complaining, the residents of Primrose Lane prepared to leave their homes on the order of the King. Discussing the situation among themselves, they felt this could only mean trouble. Some people suggested there were rumors that the King was going to have the entire neighborhood bulldozed down in their absence. Grudgingly, they began to leave – but only because they were certain that worse things would befall them if they rebelled against the evacuation order.

Yet while there was grumbling and complaining on Primrose Lane, the exact opposite was the case across town. All feelings of apprehension having been put away, faithful Kingdom citizens embraced the King's plan with enthusiasm, and could hardly wait to get started. They knew time was short. They would have to hurry. Yet they shared a common purpose and a heart to work, and depended on each other to help make the King's desire a reality. And so, laden with tools, paint, ladders, and mowers, they descended upon the neighborhood like carpenter bees. Each citizen had been given a specific assignment, and carried along the supplies to complete it. And on this special day, even the song of the birds and the humming of the bees was eclipsed by the sound of good conversation and jovial laughter.

As the first work day drew to a close, the citizens stepped back to admire their handiwork. While there were still a few touch ups to do the next day, it was clear to see a transformation was truly underway. Each house was freshly painted. Each garden neatly weeded. Every walk, porch, and fence had been repaired. Every tree and bush had been trimmed and shaped.

Candy and Eric, surveying the work that had been done, exchanged a satisfied smile. It seemed as though even the sun was shining brighter on Primrose Lane today. Gathering their tools, they bid their friends 'good night' and headed home with a feeling of total satisfaction.

"Today has been great, hasn't it?" Candy said, as she and Eric made their way down the street together.

"It certainly has," he answered, with a smile that matched hers. "I don't know when I've had a day as fulfilling as this one. The days we worked on Patty's house and lawn come close, but this has been something I really don't have words to explain."

"It was just Kingdom business, right?" Candy responded, with a peal of girlish laughter. Then added, thoughtfully, "This is how Victoria must have felt years ago each time one of us joined the tea party at the King's house. It feels so good to be doing something for someone who has no idea of the blessing that awaits them."

Without thinking, she linked arms with Eric. The children would be waiting for them, and for the dinner they hoped would soon be on the dining table. Making their way home, they reminded each other how rewarding it was to be a part of the King's plans. It felt good to put action to their decision to forgive past hurts. But what impact would their efforts have on the residents of Primrose Lane?

Candy and Eric were not the only ones with wonderment and questions in their minds that evening. One side of town was purring with the satisfaction of a job well done. However, the other side of town was brooding, certain that nothing but disappointment awaited them the next day. One group slept poorly that night, their anger building against the King and his order to evacuate their homes and leave them to his trust. The other group slept like babies, muscles sore from the day's heavy workload, but hearts filled with joy at having trusted the King and found his love faithful to all.

The next day arose with beauty all around. The sun was bright and the birds sang with anticipation of how the events of the day would unfold. As the Kingdom citizens hurried to put finishing touches on yesterday's chores, the King met with the residents of Primrose Lane.

"I wanted to meet briefly with you before you return to your homes today," he began. "I apologize for any inconvenience I may have caused you by asking you to leave for a few hours. However, there are just some projects that cannot be done amid the regular routine of life. This was one of those times. Nevertheless, I have been informed that it is now safe for you to return. So please feel free to do so at any time."

Not wanting to be recipients of the King's hospitality any longer than necessary, those from Primrose Lane quickly gathered their belongings and began to make their way home; but as they went, a constant stream of angry conversation floated with them in the air.

Following, the King slowed his pace, giving them ample time to arrive at their homes ahead of him. Before long, Victoria and Linda fell into step beside him. With an uncertain tone Linda asked, "Do you think it will work Sir?"

The King smiled as he answered her, "We will soon know, but I have found that love never fails. It is hard to be angry in the light of unconditional love." And with that remark, they picked up their pace. Something was happening ahead of them.

As each group made the turn toward Primrose Lane, the threads of their conversations died. Before long, the last of the residents stood, in amazement, at the beginning of the Primrose Lane. There was total silence. Every person had stopped …. their eyes wide and mouths dropped open.

The King, Victoria, and Linda made their way through the crowd, pausing to stand at the front of the gathering. As the three of them surveyed the crowd, it was evident that what the returning citizens saw was not at all what they had expected. Bewildered, they stared at the work that had been done, while the faithful citizens of the Kingdom approached them from the other end of the street. Now the two groups stood facing each other, waiting, uncertain how to approach, not knowing what to do.

Taking control of the situation, the King stepped forward. "Ladies and gentlemen, what you see before you is the result of unconditional love, the very fruit of a labor of love. Beloved, it has broken my heart to see you live as you have these past few years. I longed to reach out to you, and let you know that I was willing to help. But you have restricted what I could do for you. As we all know, in the past you refused to participate in the Kingdom Provision Plan. You refused to contribute because you did not trust me to look after you and care for the needs that might arise in your lives. What you see before you has been done through the fund you refused to trust. And each citizen who helped renovate and repair your homes has taken from funds they personally contributed into the trust. They wanted to share what they had with you. It was their desire – and mine – that you enjoy a better quality of life. "

As the reality of what had happened began to dawn on the residents of Primrose Lane, their first reaction was shame. Fresh in each mind and heart were the ugly, hateful words they had voiced only the night before, and how they'd believed the King intended to take their property. Now, in the light of the King's words, they realized that he had only wanted to make things better for them.

One of Patty and Ken's neighbors stepped forward. "I don't know what to say, Sir ..." he stammered. "I mean … when I saw some of the men working on Ken's place, I figured it was because they were some of the King's 'pet' citizens. I even thought it might be a trick. You know … something to make Patty forget all the bad blood between her father and the King so many years ago. But now I don't know what to think or say. Surely it must have emptied the treasuries to complete all of this work. What will the people do when trouble comes and they no longer have the reserve they had put away? Won't they turn on us and resent having done all this on our behalf?"

Linda hesitantly stepped forward. "That's the beauty of the Kingdom way of life," she began, "and it is what my husband did not want you to learn so many years ago. By not allowing the whole truth to be spoken, he robbed you of so much."

She moved forward a bit more confidently, and people began to gather around her, waiting to hear what she had to say. "Let me explain something the King has recently shared with me. When citizens obey the King's statutes and give one tenth of their earnings to the community fund controlled by the

King, he takes from his private treasures and multiplies the amount held in trust. That way no matter how great a need arises, there is always enough to meet it. The King makes up the difference ... every time! My husband feared that if you learned this truth he would lose his power over you and this neighborhood. That is why he convinced all of you that the King was evil. That is why he incited you into a fury, and why he attacked the King. Thankfully, he was not successful in killing the King. However, the bitterness and hatred he carried after that failed attempt caused him to unleash terrible anger toward Patty and myself. That's why we had to leave. Patty left while she was young enough to make a new life elsewhere. I stayed until I lost hope of her return. There was so much pain associated with this street. Yet ... thankfully ... the King never left us. He has cared for us in every way possible. He knew that even though we had never actively served him, our hearts longed to do what was right. He gave us each a fresh start, a second chance. Today, I'm asking each of you to take this second chance the King is offering. Put away old resentments and misguided ideas. Embrace the truth of the King's love and his desire to care of each of us."

Each resident of Primrose Lane looked intently into Linda's face as they listened. They had to make sure for themselves that she was speaking from her heart and not at the King's urging. One by one they made their way to the King, each one expressing sorrow over their lost years lived without him. Soon grateful hearts of thanksgiving were being lifted to the King, as each person pledged obedience to the statutes of the Kingdom. Then the two groups began mingling with one another — one group expressing their gratitude to receive such kindness, and the other group exulting in the joy of service.

Soon families began making their way toward home – bidding enthusiastic farewells to the King's helpers. How sweet and fresh the air now smelled, and how clearly the birds were suddenly singing. The afternoon sun seemed to bathe the neighborhood with a new garment of hope.

Watching them go, Victoria and the King linked arms. What joy to know that things had, once again, been made right in the Kingdom. Facing each other, their eyes spoke more than any words could ever say – for both of them knew this was the way things were meant to be.

The End.

Epilogue

*F*ollow Victoria and her friends in the upcoming sequel to *Candy* where they learn the many rewards accompanying a life lived with the Kingdom in view. Discover how simple acts of love enlarge when they are shared, how the power of words never dies, and when you think you're at "the end" ... you're not! The King never disappoints those who love his Kingdom, and continues to surprise and reward his faithful beyond comprehension.

Watch for *The Farewell* – the third installment in the *A Tea Party With The King* series.

A Note From the Author ...

*T*t is my desire that you experience the intimate presence of the King, and acquire a deeper understanding of Kingdom Business through the *A Tea Party With The King* series. If *Candy* has blessed you, I'd love to hear about it. Contact me at the address or email below, and tell me how Victoria, Candy, and their friends have touched your life.

Elizabeth Foy
Highways & Hedges Ministries
P. O. Box 825
Swartz, LA 71281
Phone 318-343-9891 or 318-282-0934
Email: highways2004@yahoo.com

LaVergne, TN USA
21 October 2010
201693LV00002B/6/P